A Trip to the Seashore

Picture yourself sitting on a large rock outcropping with the sea about 20 feet below...notice the roar as the ocean rushes in and hits the rock...smell the salt air... listen to the sea gulls chatter...notice a trail to the beach...walk down this path...take your shoes off and walk barefoot in the warm sand toward the water... dip your toes in the tepid sea...bend down and write "I love you" and the names of special people in your life ..watch as the waves carry your message out to sea. Know that your message has been delivered.

This is just one of the many visualization techniques that you will learn in this empowering book. By quieting your mind and learning to induce a state of hypnosis, you can visualize the you that you've always dreamed of—and make this a reality! Hypnosis is more than just a set of words in a relaxing procedure. It is a way to enjoy life to the fullest—a technique for creating the reality you want for yourself now and into the future.

Hypnosis for Beginners is food for your soul. It will not just feed you for a day, it will teach you how to fish for life.

About the Author

William W. Hewitt was a free-lance writer, the author of seven books and other materials published by Llewellyn Publications. He spent more than thirty years as a professional writer and editor in the computer, nuclear power, manufacturing and mining industries, and was a professional member of the National Writers Association. He was a certified clinical hypnotherapist and a professional astrologer. He lectured on hypnosis, mind power, self-improvement, metaphysics, and related subjects. He and his wife traveled extensively together after his retirement, and were a devoted couple enjoying their "golden years." He passed from this lifetime in November 2001.

Hypnosis for Beginners

Reach New Levels of Awareness & Achievement

William W. Hewitt

Llewellyn Publications
Woodbury, Minnesota

FIRST EDITION
Eleventh Printing, 2008
(previously titled *Hypnosis*)

Second edition, eleven printings, 1996. First edition, one printing, 1986

Cover design: Tom Grewe
Author's photo: Dolores Hewitt
Cover images: Paolo Galli, Jupiter Productions,
    and Digital Stock Corporation
Book design: Laura Gudbaur
Editor: Rosemary Wallner
Layout: Virginia Sutton

Library of Congress Cataloging-in-Publication Data
Hewitt, William W., 1929–2001
    Hypnosis for beginners : reach new levels of
awareness & achievement / William W. Hewitt
        p.   cm.   —(Llewellyn's beginners series)
    ISBN 13: 978-1-56718-359-7
    ISBN 10: 1-56718-359-X (pbk.)
    1. Hypnotism. 2. Autogenic training. 3. Self-actualization
(Psychology)—Miscellanea. I. Title.
II. Series.
BF1152.H575   1997
154.7--dc21   97-29024
                                                         CIP

Llewellyn Publications
A Division of Llewellyn Worldwide, Ltd.
2143 Wooddale Drive, Dept. 978-1-56718-359-7
Woodbury, Minnesota 55125-2989, U.S.A.
www.llewellyn.com
Llewellyn is a registered trademark of Llewellyn Worldwide, Ltd.
Printed in the United States of America

DEDICATION

This book is dedicated to my wife, Dee, to Carl and Sandra Weschcke, to Nancy Mostad, and to all men and women everywhere who do their very best every day to make the world a better place in which to live.

OTHER BOOKS BY THE AUTHOR

Hypnosis

Tea Leaf Reading

Astrology for Beginners

Bridges to Success & Fulfillment

The Art of Self Talk

Psychic Development for Beginners

Self-Hypnosis for a Better Life

AUDIO TAPES

Become Smoke-Free through Self-Hypnosis

Psychic Workout through Self-Hypnosis

Relaxation and Stress Management through Self-Hypnosis

Your Perfect Weight through Self-Hypnosis

Contents

Part II: Regression and Self-Regression

Part III: Practical Applications and Supplemental Information

Introduction

Hypnosis is a lot like daydreaming. When you day-dream, you alter your state of consciousness to the alpha frequency region and engage in your fantasies. All the while you are conscious and aware, yet you remain oblivious to external distractions. Daydreaming is a perfectly normal, safe, and healthy phenomenon that we all engage in from time to time. Sometimes a daydream is so intense and goal-oriented that the person achieves the goal. This usually happens spontaneously and without deliberate intent.

Hypnosis is a technique that enables you to achieve this altered state of consciousness—the daydream state—deliberately and direct your attention to specific goals in order to achieve them. Like daydreaming, hypnosis is a perfectly normal, safe, and healthy phenomenon. In hypnosis, like daydreaming, you are conscious and aware, yet remain oblivious to external distractions. In both daydreaming and hypnosis your mind adjusts to the alpha frequency range—the difference is that in hypnosis your mind is directed to specific beneficial goals you wish to achieve and not to fantasies. These beneficial goals include quitting smoking, dieting, improving self-image,

overcoming phobias and fears, improving memory—
the list of uses is limitless.

When you've completed *Hypnosis for Beginners,*
you will know how to hypnotize others or yourself for
any beneficial, worthwhile purpose. Throughout this
book, you will find complete word-by-word hypnosis
techniques and case examples to illustrate specific
points. Nothing is left for you to wonder about. You
will even learn how to modify the techniques in the
book to develop your own procedures.

If you want to learn hypnosis as part of a "get-
rich-quick" scheme or to exercise control over others,
forget it. It won't work! You will not find those procedures in this book. However, if you want to expand
your awareness, reshape and enrich your life or the
lives of others, and do so in a spirit of brotherhood and
love, then read on.

Hypnosis is one of the most valuable tools in the
world today for the enrichment of lives. With hypnosis, you can break undesirable habits, create desirable
habits, and constructively deal with and resolve every
sort of human problem. You can instill true happiness
and replace unhappiness.

If all this is true, then why isn't everyone engaged
in daily self-hypnosis? Lack of education and knowledge are the main reasons. Most people lack good
information and possess a great deal of misinforma-
tion about hypnosis. Few places offer knowledge about
hypnosis; it isn't taught in public schools and only a
handful of colleges have courses in hypnosis (and
many of these are superficial). A few commercial
schools offer hypnosis, frequently at inflated prices.

Hypnosis for Beginners includes my twenty-five years of firsthand knowledge, training, and experience gathered in a simple, lucid, and detailed presentation. This is a "how-to" book at the beginner's level; I present everything you need to know to master hypnosis and self-hypnosis. If you want to learn for your own edification, the information is here. If you want to become a professional and start a full-time or part-time business, it is here. If you want to develop the skill to help others, it is here. If you want to develop your own hypnosis techniques, it is here.

You will also find two additional bonuses in this book. First is a powerful section that teaches you how to regress into a current life as well as past lives (including exclusive scripts for performing regression on yourself). Second, this book makes you aware of how self-hypnosis can be the gateway into the realm of psychic experience.

To understand this book and master hypnosis, all you need are an average intelligence and the ability to read. That's all! No college degree. No high school diploma. No super intelligence. In fact, this book will tell you how to start developing your own super intelligence.

Hypnosis for Beginners strips away the shroud of mystery and ignorance that have cloaked hypnosis for centuries. What is left is a beautiful, powerful, simple, and natural skill for enriching the lives of all who embrace it.

No other book on the market today approaches the subject of hypnosis in the depth, the specifics of procedures, and the spirit of humanity as does this one.

MY EXPERIENCES

For over twenty-five years I have been practicing hypnosis and have hypnotized hundreds of people in almost every conceivable situation. When I first started, I practiced part time on weekends and in the evenings with no charge to my subjects, enabling me to learn and hone my hypnosis skills. During this time, I earned my living as a technical writer; because I am an altruistic person, hypnosis gave me the chance to help others.

In 1976, the demands on my time became so great that I decided to go into hypnosis full time as a business. At the time, I charged $25 per session, which was $10 to $25 per session less than most other hypnotists. (I have a fanatical dislike for greed, which explains my lower fees.) Nonetheless, in spite of high expenses (including rent, advertising, and phone charges) I did quite well.

Then two events occurred within a few months of each other that destroyed the hypnosis market in my metropolitan area. Two hypnotists (one a physician, the other a psychologist) were indicted on criminal charges in non-related cases. The physician was found guilty of massive and flagrant misuse of hypnosis for personal gain to the detriment of his patients. His medical license was revoked but no jail sentence was imposed.

In the case of the psychologist, I was the one who filed the initial charges against him with the state attorney general's office. The ensuing investigation revealed that I had only seen the tip of a huge, ugly iceberg. He was sentenced to eight years in prison.

The media coverage of these two cases was massive—and all hypnotists were tarred with the same brush. The result was that it was nearly impossible to earn a dime as a hypnotist for quite some time.

I went back to technical writing for a living while practicing hypnosis on the side once again. In 1992, I decided to retire (for the most part) and devote my time to freelance writing, giving an occasional workshop on psychic development, doing occasional hypnosis in special cases, and traveling for pleasure.

My Purpose

My purpose in writing this book is to present hypnosis as the honorable, beneficial skill that it is. Whether you practice self-hypnosis in the quiet solitude of your room or with a loved one or friend, the benefits can be enormous. A husband and wife can be drawn closer together in love, harmony, and understanding than they ever dreamed possible just by practicing hypnosis together for common goals. In self-hypnosis, you can draw closer to your higher self and through that higher self to all others—there really are no negative aspects to hypnosis. If you approach it with integrity, you reap beneficial results.

This book is divided into three parts. In Part I, you'll find out what hypnosis is, how it works, and how you can master the art of hypnosis. Chapter 1 explores the subject of hypnosis in general. You'll find a few myths about hypnosis debunked, a few do's and don'ts, and advice on initial counseling with a subject.

Chapters 2 through 6 take you through six consecutive hypnosis sessions exactly as I perform them with a client for the purpose of *diet control.* The actual hypnosis procedures are printed out in full so you can use them. (I chose diet control as an example because it makes use of most of the procedures you need. Also, diet control is a popular subject.)

In Part II, you'll learn how to perform regression and self-regression. Chapter 7 discusses using hypnosis to regress others into the past in this current life or a previous lifetime. I include the procedure I have successfully used. Chapter 8 contains the scripts that enable you to regress yourself into your own past in this life or in previous lives.

In Part III, you'll find practical applications and a variety of supplementary information. Chapter 9 is a collection of hypnotic suggestions for most of the situations you are likely to encounter. Chapter 10 discusses hypnotizing children, group hypnosis, and stage hypnosis. Chapter 11 is a collection of case histories to augment those given in other chapters. The cases selected are those that illustrate specific points about hypnosis. Chapter 12 contains additional hypnosis routines for specific purposes to augment the routines in the other chapters.

Chapter 13 deals exclusively with self-hypnosis, including how to do it to achieve virtually any goal, be it material gain, spiritual gain, healing of wounds, overcoming illness, or changing habits. This chapter brings the other chapters into sharper focus.

Chapter 14 contains detailed instructions for a broad spectrum of practical everyday applications.

Chapter 15 contains a summary of the entire subject and a brief glimpse beyond hypnosis into the area broadly defined as psychic phenomena.

THE ROUTINES

Each session in chapters 2 through 6 contains routines that are labeled with a letter, or a number and letter combination. (You do not, however, say these letters or combinations out loud. They are just for your records.) The numbering system has no special significance and is for easy identification.

When I began creating routines years ago I used all the alphabet letters and had to start incorporating numbers with some of the alphabetic numbers. It was just my system for keeping track of my work. Eventually, I eliminated some routines and combined others; the ones that were left are those in this book. I recommend that you put each routine on a separate sheet of paper or a 4 x 6 inch card. This way, you can arrange them in any order for any purpose. As you will see by the time you finish this book, you can create special procedures by putting a variety of routines in a desired order.

Italic text signifies words you speak aloud. It is good if you memorize these words, but it is perfectly all right to read them. Initially, memorize routine A (see chapter 2). It is short, and when your subject sees you are speaking from memory he tends to have more confidence in you. During routine A, you have the subject close his eyes so from that point on he doesn't know if you are reading or speaking from memory.

Reading—or not reading—aloud isn't that big of an issue anyway. You will have it all memorized after a few times. Having the routines memorized does much for your confidence in yourself also.

DEFINITION OF TERMS

Following are the definitions of several terms used throughout this book.

Operator: The hypnotist; the one who performs the hypnosis routines.

Subject: The person being hypnotized; also referred to as the client.

Gender: If the text refers to a specific case history, I use the appropriate gender (he or his; she or her). If the text does not refer to a specific case history, I use she or her. Occasionally I use "he or she" to indicate that either gender is applicable; but even when I use the female gender, the situation could equally apply to a male. The reason I use female gender is because 90 percent of my subjects have been female. In my experience, women have been more open minded and receptive to hypnosis than men have been.

Now turn the page and begin reading, enjoying, and learning a new and valuable skill. Learning hypnosis may turn out to be one of the most beneficial experiences of your life.

*P*ART *I*

Hypnosis and Self-Hypnosis

CHAPTER 1

How to Be a Hypnotist

Nearly everyone can quickly and easily learn the techniques for hypnosis and become a hypnotist. To be a good hypnotist, however, is something else. To be a good hypnotist, you need to have integrity, honesty, and dedication. You must care about humanity. Assuming you have these personal qualities, all you need to do is memorize the techniques. Then practice, practice, and more practice, and learn each time you practice. After much practice and learning, you will be able to call yourself a hypnotist.

WHAT IS HYPNOSIS?

Hypnosis is a daydream-like state. In this state, the person's conscious mind becomes quiet or passive. The hypnotist introduces suggestions into the powerful subconscious mind.

Let's take a brief, slightly technical look at how the brain operates. The brain operates on measurable frequency cycles. These frequencies correspond to certain kinds of activity.

In 1929, Hans Berger used an EEG machine to discover that when a person's eyes were closed the brain generated regular waves in the 8 to 12 cycles per second (cps) range. He labeled these brain waves *alpha waves*. Subsequently, other types of brain waves were discovered and labeled *theta, beta,* and *delta*. These brain waves have been found to correlate to various mental functions, including hypnosis and psychic experience. Experts generally agree on these brain waves and their purpose, but they disagree on the exact boundaries of each kind of wave. One expert will define alpha as 8 to 12 cps; another as 7 to 14 cps, and so forth. The next four paragraphs present a general consensus concerning these brain waves.

Delta. The frequency range of brain activity in delta ranges from 0 to about 4 cps. This is total unconsciousness. Not much is known about the delta range.

Theta. The frequency range in theta is about 4 to 7 cps. Theta is part of the subconscious range and hypnosis can sometimes take place here. All of our emotional experiences seem to be recorded in theta. Theta is that special range that opens the door of consciousness beyond hypnosis into the world of psychic phenomena. Theta is the range where psychic experience is most likely to occur (see chapter 15).

Alpha. The frequency range in alpha is about 7 to 14 cps. Alpha is usually regarded as the subconscious range. This is where dreaming (while asleep), daydreaming, and nearly all hypnosis take place. Meditation is mostly in this range (although sometimes it dips into theta). Psychic experience sometimes takes place in alpha, also. Alpha is an important region insofar as hypnosis is concerned.

Beta. This is the conscious mind region with frequency ranges from about 14 cps upward. Beta is where we do our reasoning and conduct most of our affairs while awake. For the most part, we seem to operate around 20 cps during most awake activity. At about 60 cps, a person would be in acute hysteria. Above 60 cps, I don't know what would happen; I suspect it wouldn't be pleasant.

When you go to sleep, your brain automatically cycles down from the beta range into alpha and then for brief cyclic periods into theta and delta. Most of your sleep is in alpha. Hypnosis takes advantage of this natural phenomenon—it causes the brain to cycle down into alpha without going to sleep. In alpha, the subconscious mind is open for suggestive input.

The conscious mind does not take suggestion well. It is most useful for thinking, reasoning, and putting into action those things it already knows. The subconscious mind, however, is like an obedient slave. It doesn't think or reason. It responds to what it is told. Herein lies the value and power of hypnosis. With hypnosis, you can pump powerful suggestions directly into the subconscious. The subconscious accepts these suggestions and causes them to become reality. In part, the subconscious mind informs the conscious mind that there is new information to be acted upon. The conscious mind loves to act on what it already has, so it acts on this new information. Although no one really understands why hypnosis works and how the subconscious mind brings about results, we do know it works—and works quite well.

Suggestions

You'll find the suggestions used in hypnosis in other chapters. For now, know that it is extremely important that all suggestions given are positive, constructive, and beneficial. This is because the subconscious mind doesn't know the difference between a good suggestion and a bad one. The subconscious mind merely accepts what you give it and then acts on it.

Be careful of your wording at all times while giving suggestions. One man used a slang four-letter word for defecation hundreds of times a day in his speech. Eventually, he convinced his subconscious that he wanted to defecate, and he developed chronic diarrhea. Words are powerful, and your subconscious mind takes them literally.

Myths

There are many serious misunderstandings about hypnosis. Many of these misunderstandings have been promoted by B-grade movies that depict people being transformed into zombie-like creatures by some super-powerful mystic who says, "Look into my eyes!" While this may make for an exciting movie, it is 100 percent fiction and has no resemblance to the truth. Following are some of the more common myths and their explanations.

A hypnotist has magical powers. This is completely false. A hypnotist is an ordinary human being who has mastered the skill of using the power of suggestion to bring about desired results.

A person can be hypnotized and made to do things against his or her will. Absolutely false. First, no person can be hypnotized against his or her will. The subject must be 100 percent cooperative. Second, no one under hypnosis can be made to do anything they would not freely do if not under hypnosis. During hypnosis, the subject can choose to accept or reject any suggestion given. If a suggestion is given that upsets the subject, he or she would likely come out of hypnosis immediately of their own choice.

Only weak-minded people can be hypnotized. The contrary is true. The more intelligent a person is, the easier it is to hypnotize him or her. In fact, in certain cases of mental debility, hypnosis is impossible. Nearly everyone who wants to be hypnotized, can be hypnotized. Only about 1 percent of the population cannot be hypnotized either because of mental deficiencies or reasons we don't understand.

A hypnotized person is in a trance or is unconscious. Not true at all. Under hypnosis, the subject is awake and aware—extremely so. The hypnotized subject has merely focused his or her attention to where the hypnotist directs it, and is oblivious to anything else.

A person can get stuck in hypnosis. This is completely false. Even if the operator dropped dead after putting the subject under deep hypnosis, the subject would come out of the hypnosis easily. The subject would either slip into a brief sleep and then awaken normally, or open his or her eyes when the operator's voice had not been heard for some time.

Deep hypnosis is necessary for good results. Not true. Any level of hypnosis from light to very deep can bring good results.

Hypnotic State

Under hypnosis the person is very aware of where he or she is and what is happening. The subject hears everything and is in a daydream-like state of deep relaxation. Often the subject has either a numbness throughout the body or no acute awareness of having a body.

Self-Hypnosis

It is possible to hypnotize yourself. Many people do it every day to give themselves constructive suggestions. It is much easier to hypnotize yourself if you have first been hypnotized by someone else and given the suggestion and instructions to do so. This book will teach you how to hypnotize others, and you can use the same instructions to hypnotize yourself. If you work with a partner who can hypnotize you, you will speed up your progress in learning self-hypnosis.

GOING INTO BUSINESS

If you are interested in going into business either part time or full time, the following section highlights some things you should consider in addition to the material covered in the rest of this book.

Things You Will Need

- A quiet office with a minimum of three chairs. One chair for you; a lounge chair for your subject; and a chair (optional type) for a third party. Clients frequently bring someone with them. If you use a room in your home, you'll save rent money and give yourself a tax write-off. If you rent an office, find one that is quiet, has ample parking, and has easy driving access from all directions.

- A desk or table for writing.

- A cassette tape recorder and a supply of blank tapes.

- Paper, folders, and file space for record keeping.

- A supply of printed self-hypnosis instructions (see chapter 3).

- A supply of printed diet sheets (see chapter 3).

- Two pen lights with fresh batteries. You need these only if you read the induction procedures and the room is too dimly lit for reading.

- A 6 x 6 inch (approximate size) card with a large, solid red dot drawn on it (see chapter 3).

- All of your hypnosis routines typed up and handy for quick access in case you have a brief memory lapse. Even after I had memorized hypnosis routines, I still kept the printed routines (one routine per 4 x 6 inch card) readily available as a security blanket. If you don't want to type up the routines, buy two more copies of this book and cut out the routines and paste or tape them onto cards. Two books are necessary because many of the routines are printed back to back on the same page. The low cost of two more books certainly offsets the drudgery of all that typing.

- Release forms. These are to be signed by your clients attesting that they understand the nature of hypnosis, enter it willingly, and release you from any guarantees or liabilities. Consult with your attorney about actual wording of a release form.

- Business cards

- Telephone

- Either a receptionist with an outer office or a recorder to answer your phone when you are giving an induction.

Expenses

- Rent (unless you work out of your home)

- Advertising. This is expensive, but necessary to some degree. One display ad (perhaps 3 x 4 inches) in the Sunday newspaper is about as much as you need to spend. If you sign a long-term contract, you may be able to get a lower rate. A *must* is a small display ad in the yellow pages of the phone directory. About 70 percent of my business came from the yellow pages; 20 percent from word-of-mouth; and 10 percent from the newspaper.

Accept every invitation you can to speak about hypnosis, including gatherings of local clubs, high school or college classes, and house parties. These speaking engagements act as excellent advertisements.

Charges

When I retired in 1992, I was charging $50 per session (a session lasts from 30 minutes to an hour). I do not go beyond one hour because I find that too much time in one session becomes counter-productive for the client. The charge includes everything: pre- and post-hypnosis consultation, the hypnosis session, a tape recording of one of the sessions (usually session 5), and the self-hypnosis handouts. If I make an office or house call, I charge a modest fee for travel time and gasoline if it is over five miles one way.

In some parts of the country (including large metropolitan areas), a charge of $50 to $100 per session might be reasonable. A charge of $20 to $40 per session might be more appropriate for small towns or rural areas. Evaluate your own situation and set fees accordingly.

My philosophy is that you charge the very least you can and still pay your expenses and give yourself a reasonable return for your time and skill.

Try to give a client the fewest possible sessions to achieve the desired goal. I never will allow a client to see me for more than six sessions. This is because I want to help a client to be independent and solve his or her own problems. I do not want the client to be dependent on me. I teach the client self-hypnosis starting on the second session so he or she will have the tools to solve problems just as effectively as I can solve them. I recommend you take a similar approach in your hypnosis practice. Don't get greedy. Think of your client's needs first. You will make out okay.

I strongly recommend that you request payment *in advance* for each session. Once you give the session, you cannot take it back if the client doesn't pay or writes a bad check. You may want to give a price break incentive for pre-payment. For example, pay for five sessions on your first visit, and get the sixth one free.

HOW TO PERFORM HYPNOSIS

First, you must have the hypnosis routines either memorized or typed and handy so you can easily read them. Next come a myriad of things to consider, including tone of voice and pace of speech; position of yourself and your subject; environment (including lighting, noise, and background sounds); recording sessions; use of external equipment; observing your subject; and testing for results.

Tone and Pace

Use the voice you were born with. That may sound like a stupid statement, but it isn't. I have seen many beginning hypnotists deliberately alter their voices when performing to try to have a more resonant, deep, theatrical sound. This is nonsense. Use your normal speaking voice. A beautiful, melodic, resonant voice is certainly an asset, but it is not necessary. It is more important to know what you are doing and have a good rapport with and respect for your subject than to have a resonant speaking voice.

You do, however, need to practice the pace of your speech. Your speech pattern should be slow enough to give the subject time to respond to your directions and yet fast enough to retain her attention and interest. If you go too slow, the subject's mind might wander to other thoughts; you want to maintain the subject's attention to your voice. Some people may need a faster pace while others need a slower pace. Experience will help you find just the right pace.

A pause of two to five seconds is a good average. For example: *relax your knees* (two-second pause); *relax your calves* (two-second pause); *and now relax your toes* (one-second pause); *relax your toes* (two-second pause).

In some visualization routines you may need longer pauses. For example: *I want you to imagine now that you are standing at the top of a spiral staircase* (three-second pause); *create the staircase* (three-second pause); *it is carpeted. Create the carpet* (three-second pause).

Do not use your watch for timing these pauses; develop a feel for the timing. When I conduct hypnosis, I perform the instructions myself as I give them, thereby keeping a comfortable pace.

Speak in a rather dull, monotonous voice. The idea is to bore the subject's conscious mind to the point that it stops being active, allowing the subconscious mind to be accessible and receptive to your suggestions. If there is too much inflection or drama in your voice, the subject's conscious mind tends to retain interest, thus remaining active and thwarting your goal of deep relaxation and susceptibility to suggestion.

Physical Positioning

You can perform hypnosis while sitting or standing. Your subjects may recline in a comfortable chair, sit in straight-backed chair, lie in bed or on the floor, sit cross-legged on the floor, or stand. All positions work fine, but not necessarily for all situations. For example, a quick two-minute procedure to relieve pain works fine on a person who is standing up, but a thirty-minute procedure for diet control is out of the question for a person who is standing up.

A recliner chair or straight-backed, armless chair are the best choices for the subject. Both offer sufficient comfort and support, and the subject will rarely drift into sleep in either of these. I prefer my subjects to be in a recliner chair. However, for self-hypnosis I much prefer to be in a straight-backed, armless chair. As the operator, I also prefer a straight-backed, armless chair.

Lying in bed also offers comfort and support for the subject. The drawback is that the subject might easily drift into sleep. The body and mind have been conditioned to go to sleep when the person lies down and the brain reaches alpha. A skilled operator can usually avoid this happening. When you are working with bedridden people, this is the physical position you must deal with.

Lying on the floor has the same drawback as lying in bed: The subject is more likely to fall asleep. In addition, the floor tends to become uncomfortable rather quickly so I do not recommend it for lengthy procedures.

Sitting cross-legged on the floor also tends to become uncomfortable so I do not recommend it for lengthy procedures either. I use this position for myself for meditation (a form of self-hypnosis) and have had excellent results. I once was in deep meditation for one-and-a-half hours in this position without having any physical discomfort. I doubt that an untrained, unskilled person could do that and still be able to get up, much less walk.

Typically, my subject will be in a recliner chair. I will be sitting in a straight-backed chair facing her. The distance between is from 2 to 6 feet. There may or may not be a table or desk between us; this isn't important one way or the other. I position myself close enough to my subject so I can speak normally and be easily heard, yet far enough so as to not intimidate her. For some procedures I use for special occasions, I need to stand immediately in front of the subject or have physical contact with the subject. These are the exception, not the rule.

Ideally, the subject's chair should be placed so that no bright light falls on her eyes. Have windows (unless heavily draped) and lights to her back. This makes it easier for her to relax and be comfortable.

Where to Conduct Hypnosis

You can conduct hypnosis just about anywhere, including dimly lit rooms, bright sunlight outdoors, in quiet, and in noise. The ideal place, however, is a quiet, comfortable room with subdued lighting.

If unplanned distractions occur, use them to your advantage. Once I had just begun the hypnosis induction when a carpenter in the adjacent office began hammering nails in the wall right behind my subject's head. It was a staccato bang, bang, bang, bang. I abandoned my usual induction routine and improvised. I said, *Outside noises will not distract you. In fact outside noises will help you to reach a deeper, healthier state of relaxation.* Then as each "bang" occurred I said, *Go deeper* (bang); *deeper* (bang); *deeper and deeper* (bang). My subject went into deep relaxation as though she was on a fast down elevator. I didn't even need to continue with the remainder of my planned routines. I immediately began giving the suggestions and then brought her out. The results were excellent.

Background Music

Many hypnotists regularly have soothing music or a special tape of the ocean's surf playing in the background while they perform the induction. I have tried both the music and the surf and found them to be satisfactory. However, I have had just as satisfactory results without the background noise. Try it both ways and see which you prefer.

Auxiliary Equipment

All you really need is an inexpensive portable cassette recorder. I use this only to record one of the induction procedures while I am giving it. I then give the tape to the subject to keep (see chapter 6). If you decide to use background sounds, you will need the equipment for that.

Some hypnotists use an electric shock device to

condition their subjects. For example, during the suggestion phase of the procedure the operator might say, *Imagine now that you are smoking a cigarette. Take a deep drag.* (Then he would press the button and give the subject an electrical shock). This way the subject equates smoking to a painful experience. I am adamantly opposed to such procedures and devices. They can be dangerous and harmful, and are totally unnecessary. A good hypnotist can achieve the same result without resorting to such measures. I once took over an office that had one of these machines. I refused to accept it as part of the inventory and wouldn't sign until it had been physically removed from the premises. My advice: AVOID ANY SUCH APPARATUS COMPLETELY. They are bad news.

Observing the Subject

The key items you look for are breathing patterns and muscle tone. As the subject slips into deep relaxation, breathing will be easy and rhythmic. There will be an occasional very deep breath with easy exhaling.

Watch the hands of your subject. Are they gripping the arms of the chair? fidgeting? twitching? or are they resting without apparent tenseness?

The head should droop as the neck muscles relax. The jaw should slacken. There should be no signs of muscle strain or tenseness.

The eyelids may flutter. This is not tenseness but rather an indication that the subject is in a state called REM, or rapid eye movement. This state occurs at about 10 cycles per second of brain activity, which is well within the alpha range. If you observe REM, you know for sure that your subject is in hypnosis. The subject can be in hypnosis without REM, so don't be concerned if you do not observe it.

In general, look for signs of relaxation to indicate that the subject is in hypnosis. Signs of nervousness or tenseness indicate she probably is not in hypnosis or at most only on the edge of hypnosis.

Do not get overly concerned if a subject doesn't appear to be relaxing very much. No two people react exactly the same way to hypnosis. Just continue executing your hypnosis routines; they will work in all but a few cases.

I have had subjects who became as limp as wet dishrags within moments after I've started the induction. Others have fidgeted through most of the first session before relaxing only slightly. A few didn't really start to relax until the second session. I have had only one subject that I was unable to hypnotize. After three sessions, she was still tense and high strung. I gave her a complete refund and sent her to a colleague (who had the same unsatisfactory results).

The best indicator of a subject's responsiveness to hypnosis is to question her about it after you have brought her out of the hypnosis. The subject will tell you whether she was relaxed or not and exactly what she experienced. Of course, final results are the absolute indicator. If you are hypnotizing to stop smoking, and the subject stops, you know you performed your skill correctly and the subject was responsive.

Testing

Some hypnotists perform little tests during the induction to see if the hypnosis is working. For example, they might tell the subject to try to raise her arm just after telling her, "Your arm is like a log, stiff, immovable." If she raises her arm, she isn't under hypnosis yet. If she doesn't raise her arm, the induction has produced some level of hypnosis.

I do not do testing at all. My theory is that testing creates a doubt in the subject's mind. The subject might begin to think "Isn't he sure about what he is doing?" "Maybe I am not a good hypnosis subject?" "Will it work or not?" Besides, what will you do if the test fails and she raises her arm? The only thing you can do is continue the induction, which you were going to do anyway. Have confidence: The induction *does* work. And lo and behold, *it does.*

PRE-HYPNOSIS CONSULTATION

The pre-hypnosis consultation usually immediately precedes hypnosis session 1, which is covered in the next chapter. The consultation is extremely important and should not be skipped. (For self-hypnosis, a type of pre-hypnosis consultation is also recommended; see chapter 13.)

The purpose of the consultation is many faceted. It is the time when you explain what hypnosis is to your subject and answer any questions that may arise. It gives you the opportunity to establish a rapport with the subject, gain her confidence, and have the subject perform several simple exercises to put her at ease. There are a number of key questions you need to ask the subject to determine whether or not you wish to proceed with the actual hypnosis.

If the subject is apprehensive about being hypnotized (after you have thoroughly explained the hypnosis program), *don't attempt to hypnotize her.* Ask her to think about it for a few days. Let her know that you will be happy to answer any questions.

Conversely, if your subject wants to be hypnotized, but you have reservations, don't do it. It is vitally important that you and your subject have a mutual rapport and understanding if you are to have a successful program. Always keep in mind that the goal of hypnosis is to help someone gain more control over his or her life and to improve the quality of that life in some manner. This is difficult to achieve if obstacles (such as lack of trust, poor rapport, and apprehension toward each other) stand between the operator and the subject.

Do not hesitate to refuse hypnosis. A woman came to my office to begin a series of six sessions for diet control. In our pre-hypnosis consultation, my sixth sense told me that something was seriously inharmonious between us. Under gentle questioning, the woman admitted a deep hatred and mistrust of men in general. She quickly said, "I won't allow that to interfere with anything, though." Of course, I realized her good intentions weren't good enough. She needed help more with her hatred than with diet control, and only someone for whom she had complete respect could help her. I refused to take her as a client.

Instead, I set up an appointment for her to see a colleague, a female hypnotist, for consultation. The woman had a successful program with my colleague, conquering both her hatred and her eating compulsion, and she phoned to thank me. No doubt she would have gone to the female hypnotist in the first place had she known about her. Again, always do what is best for the subject even if it deprives you of a fee or an interesting experience.

IMPORTANT: *If you suspect a mental or health problem, do not attempt to deal with it.* Refuse to take the person as a client until he or she has seen a physician and the physician sanctions the hypnosis treatment. Also, do not accept a client whom you know or strongly suspect is on illegal drugs. The grief you can create for yourself can be a lifelong nightmare.

Consultation Scenario

The consultation should go something like this:

First, have the subject fill out and sign a brief fact sheet that includes name, address, phone number, purpose in wanting hypnosis, name he or she prefers to be called, and any other data you may deem pertinent. I usually keep this brief, preferring to elicit the data from the subject during discussion and making my own notes.

Second, ask why the subject wants hypnosis. Take your time exploring this thoroughly. Frequently, the reason given is not the real problem. If the answer is for diet control, find out what she has done in the past for diet. Does she have a health problem? Is she under a doctor's care? Is she taking medication or drugs? If so, what kind? why? Is it under a doctor's care? Do not leave this subject until you are comfortable with the answers.

Third, explain thoroughly what hypnosis is and isn't. Allay all apprehensions. Invite questions. Explain your entire six-session program and your fees. Stress that there are no guarantees; the results depend on her responsiveness. Stress also that she cannot be made to do anything under hypnosis that is contrary to her will. She cannot be made to do anything that she wouldn't be willing to do while not under hypnosis. Also stress that she will always be aware of everything that is happening and will remember everything that happened.

Fourth, give a mini-demonstration of two pre-hypnosis training exercises to show how simple hypnosis is. (These two exercises are detailed later in this chapter.)

Fifth, begin with hypnosis session 1.

The preceding five steps are a suggested outline for your consultation. In practice, you will develop your own style and sequence. Three important things to achieve regardless of your structure are: 1) inform the subject completely about you and hypnosis; 2) inform yourself completely about the subject; and 3) establish a comfortable rapport between you and the subject.

Problem Areas

Medical care. If the subject is under medical care, do not do anything to interfere with that. Unless you are a medical doctor (few doctors know or practice hypnosis), do not play doctor; that is not your role and could be detrimental to your subject. In cases where the subject has a medical situation, I always ask permission to consult with the subject's physician. If the subject says no, I do not do the hypnosis. If the subject says yes, I then am guided by the results of my consultation with her physician.

Find the true reason. Frequently the reason given for wanting hypnosis is not really the problem that needs to be dealt with. Here is one of my cases that illustrates the point rather humorously: An attractive, middle-aged woman came to me ostensibly for diet control. She didn't appear to me to have a weight problem, but I nevertheless went through a complete consultation with her, explaining all about hypnosis and about my diet control program. After my explanation, she still was apprehensive about hypnosis. So I continued questioning until she finally admitted that she was concerned that I would take sexual advantage of her while she was hypnotized. I assured her quite firmly, "You will be aware at all times, and I cannot make you do anything under hypnosis that you would not do willingly while not under hypnosis. She smiled weakly and muttered, *"That's the problem!"*

A few years ago I stopped doing hypnosis specifically for diet control, smoking, or phobias. I began dealing only with self-image improvement and handling of stress. I find these two items to be at the root of all problems. Of course, I may put in a suggestion or two about not smoking, or regulating appetite, but my main thrust is self-image improvement and/or stress control. I find that when one's self-image is healthy and balanced, problems go away or are handled satisfactorily.

Keep calm. Occasionally, bizarre things can happen and you must be ready to handle them in a calm, confident, mature manner. You must never let your subject think that you are not absolutely in command. You must never appear to be rattled, upset, or confused, and you must never scold the subject or express disappointment at their response. Whatever the subject does or says is the way it is, so you as the operator must learn to accept that and deal with it.

You must never, I repeat *never,* be judgmental. If the topic of abortion makes you see red, and you are a staunch anti-abortionist, do not attempt to help the young, unmarried woman who is experiencing deep guilt over having had an abortion. Your own feelings might well cause you to intensify the woman's guilt rather than help her handle it.

Here is the most bizarre situation I've encountered and how I handled it: A middle-aged woman burst into my office in hysteria. She was crying, screaming, and babbling incoherently. Fortunately, I had an hour until my next appointment. My wife, who was my receptionist, and I gently led her to one of my lounge chairs, and I asked her to sit down. I sat across from her and said nothing. I let her cry and babble until she was exhausted. In her babbling, I got enough of her story to know that she was suicidal and en route to killing herself when she came to my office.

The details of why she was going to kill herself aren't germane to this example; her life was a colossal mess. When she finally grew tired she said, "I'm sorry I have bothered you. I know there is no way you can hypnotize me or help me while I am in this condition."

"Let's just talk about it," I said. "Your eyes are all red; they must burn." She nodded yes. "Why not just close your eyes and rest them while we talk." She did, and I had her under hypnosis within minutes without her realizing it. My purpose was to get her to commit to herself under hypnosis to live for two more weeks while giving me a chance to help her. The story has a happy ending. After four sessions in two weeks, she had rejected the thought of suicide and started to exercise her option to live. Over the subsequent weeks she very nicely restructured her life.

Forgetting the words. If you forget what you are supposed to say while hypnotizing a subject, don't panic, stammer, or apologize. Just pause briefly and then say something like, "Just go on relaxing, deeper and deeper with each breath." In a moment, you will recall your lines (or find your nearby paper with the words on it). In the meantime, improvise in a soft, slow, confident manner.

Infatuation. The bond between the operator and the subject grows very strong very quickly. Occasionally, the subject interprets that bond as something stronger and more personal.

Be forewarned that your subject may become infatuated with you. This is something you will have to handle in your own way. You must be firm without creating a feeling that you are rejecting the person. It is sound practice to not socialize with your subject, not even a casual luncheon date. When I've had an over-zealous subject try to get too familiar with me, I remind her that my wife is the receptionist. That has always thrown cold water on the situation. I highly recommend that if you are in this business you have your husband or wife as the receptionist. If you are not in business but practice hypnosis as a hobby, try to have a third person present. Otherwise, you are on your own and may find yourself in an uncomfortable situation.

Dependency. Another problem that can grow out of this strong bond is that of dependency. As an operator, you use hypnosis to enable a person to become more independent; and this is nearly always the results. Once in awhile, however, a subject finds it comfortable to lean on the "strong, confident, all-knowing" operator. When this happens, you must wean them quickly for your sake as well as theirs.

Here is one situation I encountered: Ms. X was a model who was fearful of virtually everything. She was the ex-mistress of a local mobster who was slain just minutes after she had left his house, so she feared for her life also. Her parents had been domineering while she was a youth and never allowed her to make even the simplest decisions. Her parents told her what to do. Her agent told her what to do. Her mobster boyfriend had told her what to do. She had never lived for herself.

Then she came to me, and through hypnosis she learned how to be free. Free to live. Free to have courage. It was a great experience for her, and she didn't want to let go. After our six sessions were completed, she phoned me at the office during the day and at home at night. The first few times I was tolerant. Then I politely told her to stop calling. After about two weeks of futile attempts, I coldly told her to never call me again; if she did I would hang up and not talk. She cried, of course, but she mended quickly and went on to pursue a successful life on her own. She knew how, but didn't want to give up her security blanket. Sometimes you must take a firm stance for your subject's sake as well as yours. Another rule: *Never allow your subject to get the upper hand or tell you what to do.*

Unplanned responses. Do not allow unplanned responses to sidetrack you. Once I was hypnotizing a woman for the first time. At a point in the procedure I said, "Your arms are now like logs. Stiff. Numb. Simply immovable." She immediately broke into an ear-to-ear grin and began giggling. Her eyes remained closed, but she chuckled for a minute or so. I was curious as to why this was happening, but I ignored it. I just continued to monotonously speak the words to take her into deeper relaxation. Later, when the session was over she explained that her intent was to wave both arms vigorously in the air when I said they were immovable and loudly proclaim, "See, it's not working!" But she was unable to lift her arms. It struck her as silly that she could be aware of who she was, sitting unrestrained in the chair, and yet not be able to move her arms simply because I had said she couldn't move them. That explained her grin and giggling.

Pre-Hypnosis Exercises

Following are two pre-hypnosis exercises. Use them during your consultation period to familiarize your subject with hypnosis and put her at ease. The italicized words are the ones you say. (You'll find self-hypnosis exercises in chapter 13.)

Exercise 1: *I want you to close your eyes now for a brief exercise. I want you to picture a chalkboard in your mind. Create the chalkboard. It can be black or green or whatever color you wish. Create it. It has a chalk tray with chalk and an eraser in it. Do you have it?*

(Wait for a response. When you get a yes response, proceed.)

Fine. Now take a piece of chalk and draw a circle on your board. Do you have the circle?

(Wait for yes, then proceed).

Good. Now print the letter A inside the circle. Do you have A in the circle?

(Wait for yes, then proceed).

Now erase the A from inside the circle, but don't erase the circle. Say okay when you have done that.

(Wait for okay).

Very good. Now erase the circle and open your eyes.

At this point you may have a brief dialog with the subject about her experience with the chalkboard. Assure her that whatever her experience was, it was fine. Each person responds differently. Some actually see the board. Others sense it. Others know intellectually that it is there. All responses are correct. There are no wrong experiences in hypnosis; whatever you experience is the way it is for you, and it is all right. Make a point of telling the subject that this sort of response happens frequently in hypnosis.

Exercise 2: *Close your eyes again for one more training exercise. This time I want you to focus your attention on the tip of your nose. Are you doing this?*

Wait for yes, then proceed.

Good. Keep your attention focused gently and casually on the tip of your nose and go on listening to the sound of my voice. In some of the hypnosis techniques we will be doing together, I will ask you to focus your attention on the tip of your nose in order to intensify your concentration and deepen your state of relaxation. If at any time during hypnosis you find your mind wandering, all you need to do is focus your attention on the tip of your nose as you are doing now and your mind will stop wandering and will once again follow my voice. Now you may open your eyes.

You may have a brief dialog about this exercise, then you are ready to begin hypnosis session 1 as detailed in the next chapter.

CHAPTER 2

Hypnosis Session 1

This session is an excellent sequence of routines for testing a subject's responsiveness to the operator (you) and getting the subject acclimated to the hypnosis procedures.

SESSION 1 consists of 12 routines in the following sequence: A, 1A, B, 1B, 1C, 1D, 1E, 1F, 1G, 1H, 1I, 1J.

Just before starting session 1, give the following brief instruction to the subject:

In a few moments I am going to ask you to close your eyes and follow my instructions. Shortly after we begin the session, I will ask you on three separate occasions to open your eyes. When I do ask, I really do not want you to open your eyes. I want you to pretend to try to open your eyes by stretching the eyelids, but I do not want you to open them. Then I will say something like, "Now relax your eyes," at which time you may stop pretending to try to open them and just relax. Here is what I mean.

(I demonstrate what I mean.)

Now you try it.

(I wait for a few moments to allow the subject to do with his eyelids what I just demonstrated.)

That was fine. Of course, at the very end of this session I will really want you to open your eyes when I say something like "In a few moments I will count from one to five and you will open your eyes and be wide awake." Do you understand? In the beginning we will have three brief tests where I do not want you to open your eyes, but at the very end of the session I really do want you to open them.

(I wait for the subject to acknowledge that he understands. If he doesn't, I go over it until he does.)

Now let's begin.

ROUTINE A

First I want you to stand up and take a good, complete stretch. Get all the kinks out.

(I wait for a few moments while the subject stands up and stretches thoroughly.)

That's fine. Now just sit in the chair and relax. Close your eyes and take a nice deep, full breath and exhale completely, all the way to the bottom of your lungs. All out. Do it again now. Just relax and let it all out. One more time, and this time hold your breath when you have filled your lungs with clean, refreshing, relaxing air. Hold it in. Keep your eyes closed. Now let your breath out slowly and feel yourself relaxing all over.

ROUTINE 1A

Focus your attention on your knees now and relax everything below your knees. Relax your calves. Relax your ankles. Relax your feet. And relax your toes. Relax your toes. Everything below your knees now are loose and relaxed. Now relax your thighs as completely as you can. Let your thighs just droop limp and loose and heavy into the chair. Relax your hips and relax your waist. Now relax your chest as completely as you can. Allow your breathing to be easier and deeper, more regular and more relaxed. Relax your shoulders now. Let the muscles in your shoulders be heavy and loose. More and more completely relaxed. Relax your neck and throat. Let your head just droop as all the muscles in your neck just relax. Now relax your face as completely as you can. Allow your face to be smooth and loose, relaxed and easy, your jaws all loose and relaxed, your teeth are not quite touching. Everything smooth and loose and easy. Now relax as completely as you can all the little muscles around your eyelids. Feel your eyelids growing heavier and smoother. More and more deeply relaxed.

In a moment, I am going to ask you to open your eyelids. When I ask you to open them, your eyelids will be so relaxed and heavy they will just barely open and when I ask you to close your eyelids again you will allow yourself to relax even more completely. Now try to open your eyelids. Now close your eyes and feel yourself relaxing even more.

Routine B

I want you to imagine now that all your tensions, all your tightness, and all your fears and worries are draining away from the top of your head. Let it drain down through your face, down through your neck, through your shoulders, through your chest, your waist, your hips, your thighs, down through your knees, your calves, your ankles, your feet, and out your toes. All your tension, all your tightness, all your worries and fears are draining away now from the very tips of your toes, and you are relaxing more and more.

Routine 1B

We are going to do this relaxation exercise again. This time I want you to allow yourself to relax even more fully and completely than you did the first time.

Focus your attention on your knees once again and relax everything below your knees. Relax your calves. Relax your ankles. Relax your feet, and relax your toes. And now relax your thighs even more completely. Allow your thighs to droop limp and heavy into the chair. Relax your hips and your waist. Feel the relaxation flowing into your chest now. Relaxing the vital organs within your chest, your heart, your lungs, allowing your breathing to be more intense, more regular, more and more completely relaxed. Now relax your shoulders even more. Feel your shoulders heavy and loose. More and more deeply relaxed. Relax your neck and throat. Relax your face even more. Feel your face all smooth and loose, completely easy and relaxed all over. And now relax even more all the little muscles around your eyelids. Feel your eyelids heavy and smooth, more and more deeply relaxed.

In a moment when I ask you to open your eyelids, your eyelids will be so relaxed, so lazy, that they may not even work. But whether your eyelids open or whether they do not open, in either case when I ask you to close your eyes again you will allow yourself to relax even more completely. Open your eyelids. Now close your eyes, and feel yourself relaxing even more.

ROUTINE 1C

We are going to do this relaxation exercise once again. This time I want you to allow yourself to relax completely. There is nothing to fear, you will always hear me, so just pull out all the stops and allow yourself to sink into perfect relaxation.

Focus your attention again upon your knees and relax everything below your knees. Relax your calves, relax your ankles, relax your feet, and relax your toes. Now relax your thighs completely. Feel the deep and heavy relaxation flowing into your hips now. Feel it going up through your waist, flowing into your chest, to your shoulders, heavy and loose, completely relaxed. And now this heavy relaxed feeling is going into your neck and throat, all over your face. Your face is all smooth and loose, completely easy and relaxed, and the heavy relaxation is flowing into your eyes and eyelids now. Your eyelids are so heavy and so smooth. Ever more deeply relaxed.

Routine 1D

In a moment when I ask you to open your eyelids, I want you to believe very very strongly that your eyelids are glued together. I want you to imagine that your eyelids are one piece of skin. Like one piece of skin. Don't be antagonistic or skeptical and say that you can open your eyelids. Just believe, just imagine that your eyelids are glued together. And if you believe and if you imagine that you cannot open your eyelids, you will really not be able to open them. Believe now very very strongly that your eyelids are glued together. Imagine your eyelids are like one piece of skin. Now try to open your eyes. Now let your eyes relax. Feel yourself relaxing all over.

Routine 1E

I want you to imagine now that you are looking at a blackboard. And on the blackboard is a circle. Into the circle put an X. And now erase the X from inside the circle. And now erase the circle. Forget about the blackboard now as you just go on relaxing more and more deeply.

In a moment, I am going to count backward from 100. I want you to count with me silently to yourself. Say each number to yourself as I say it, then when I ask you, erase the number from your mind and allow yourself to relax even more deeply. 100...say the 100 to yourself. Now erase it from your mind and go deeper. 99...and erase it all away. 98 and erase it. 97 and now erase it so completely there is nothing left at all, just deeper and deeper waves of relaxation.

ROUTINE 1F

Focus your attention now on the very tip of your nose just as we practiced before. Keep your attention gently focused on the tip of your nose until you reach a point where your entire attention is on my voice. And when you reach that point, you can forget about your nose and just go on listening to my voice and allowing yourself to relax more and more deeply. And as you keep your attention focused very gently on the tip of your nose I am going to take you down through four progressively deeper levels of relaxation.

ROUTINE 1G

I will label these levels with letters of the alphabet, and when you reach the first level, level A, you will be ten times more deeply relaxed than you are even now. And then from level A we will go down to level B, and when you reach level B you will be ten times again more deeply relaxed than you were before. And from level B we will go down even further, down to level C. And when you reach level C you will be ten times again more deeply relaxed than before. And then from level C we will go all the way down to the deepest level of relaxation, level D. And when you reach level D, you will be ten times again more deeply relaxed than before. You are drifting down now, two times deeper with each breath that you exhale. Two times deeper with each breath. Your hands and fingers are so relaxed and heavy, and they keep growing heavier. Feel the heaviness growing in your hands and fingers. Heavy...heavier still until now they are so heavy it is as though your hands and fingers were made of lead. And this deep relaxed, heavy feeling is flowing up through your forearms now. Feel it going up into your upper arms. Flowing through your shoulders, into your neck, over your face, over your eyes. Flowing up to your eyebrows, your forehead, over the top of your head. The deep relaxed, heavy feeling is flowing down the back of your head and down the back of your neck. You are now approaching level A.

ROUTINE 1H

You are on level A now and still going deeper. Five times deeper now with each breath that you exhale. Five times deeper with each breath. Your mind is so still and peaceful. You're not thinking of anything now. Too relaxed to think. Too comfortable to think. And this heavy relaxation in your mind is flowing into your face and eyes. It is flowing down through your neck and into your chest. Flowing down to your waist, down through your hips, your thighs, your knees, your calves, your ankles, your feet and your toes. You are now approaching level B.

ROUTINE 1I

You are on level B now and still drifting deeper. Floating smoothly and gently into perfect relaxation. Your arms and legs are so relaxed and heavy they feel like logs. Your arms and legs are stiff and numb and heavy...simply immovable. Your arms and legs are like planks of wood. You are now approaching level C.

You are on level C now and still drifting down. Sinking into the chair. Sinking deeper and deeper into perfect relaxation. And as you go on drifting even deeper, I am going to count backward from 15 to 1. Each number that I say will take you deeper and deeper still, and when I reach 1 you will be on level D. 15, deeper, 14, deeper still, 13...12...11...10...9...8...7...6, let it all go now, 5...4...3...2...1...1...1, so deep, so dreamy, so heavy, so misty. You are now on level D and still drifting down. There is no limit now...no limit. Go on floating, drifting deeper and deeper into perfect relaxation, deeper with each breath.

At this point, give your suggestions. If I use this session as the only session I plan with a client, the suggestions will be as extensive as necessary for the problem being handled. Usually this session is just the first of four or six planned for handling problem. In this case, I just put in a few general welfare suggestions such as the following:

This is the first of a series of hypnosis sessions that will enable you to get more control of your life and to enrich your life by solving your problems.

Repeat the following statements to yourself as I say them: "Every day in every way, I am getting better, better, and better."

Positive thoughts bring me benefits and advantages I desire.

Use the above suggestions or tailor your own. But you should put at least one suggestion in and probably no more than three at this point. Then proceed to the closing routine, 1J.

Routine 1J

The next time I see you, or whenever you hear my voice on tape, you will allow yourself to relax ten times more deeply than you are now. And the suggestions I give you then will go ten times deeper into your mind.

In a few moments I will awaken you. When you awaken you will feel very relaxed and very refreshed all over. You will feel alive and alert, very refreshed. Full of energy. You will feel just wonderful. You will keep on feeling relaxed and fine all the rest of today, and all this evening. Tonight when you are ready to go to sleep, you will sleep just like a log all night long. And the first thing you know it will be morning, and you will awaken feeling on top of the world.

I am now going to count from 1 to 5. At the count of 5 you will open your eyes, be wide awake and feeling fine, feeling relaxed, refreshed, alert, and in very high spirits. Feeling simply terrific!

1...2...coming up slowly now...3...at the count of 5 you will open your eyes, be wide awake and feeling fine, feeling better than before...4...5. (Here I usually snap my fingers at the count of 5 and say:) *Open eyes, wide awake and feeling fine, feeling better than before, and this is so!*

Things to Note About Session 1

Look over routines 1A, 1B, and 1C. At a quick glance, they seem to be the same. A closer look reveals subtle differences in the wording; these differences are very important. We progress from telling the subject to relax, to feeling the relaxation, to you are now relaxed.

Routine 1J uses the words "or whenever you hear my voice on tape." If you are not going to tape any sessions, omit this. If you think you might perform relaxation over the telephone, add "or whenever you hear my voice on the telephone" to pre-condition your subject for future sessions.

CHAPTER 3

Hypnosis Session 2

In this session we really get down to business and achieve two goals: To begin specific routines and suggestions to deal with the diet and eating habits (or whatever the problem), and teach the subject self-hypnosis.

SESSION 2 consists of 16 routines in the following sequence: A, B, C, D, E, F, G, H, J, K, L, M, N, O, P, Q.
Routines A and B are found in chapter 2.

ROUTINE C

Focus your attention on your toes now and allow your toes to relax completely. Each toe is loose and heavy. Now let this relaxation flow into your feet, into your ankles, your calves, your knees. Feel it flowing into your thighs, into your hips, into your waist, flowing up into your chest now. Feel your breathing easier and deeper, more regular and more relaxed. Now let the deep relaxed feeling go into your shoulders, down your arms, into your upper arms, your forearms, and into your hands and fingers, and flowing back into your forearms, your upper arms, your shoulders. Flowing into your neck, over your face, your chin, your cheeks, even your ears are relaxed. Feel it flowing into your eyes and eyelids now Your eyelids are so heavy and smooth. Flowing up into your eyebrows, over your fore- head, over the top of your head, down the back of your head, and down the back of your neck.

ROUTINE D

A new heaviness is starting in your toes now. Twice as heavy as the first time. Imagine a heavy weight on each toe. Feel the heaviness deep and even more relaxed. And this heavy, deep feeling is going into your feet, your ankles, your calves, your knees, going into your thighs, your hips, into your waist. Flowing up into your chest now, relaxing your heart, relaxing your lungs, allowing your breathing to be more intense, more regular, more and more completely relaxed. Now the deep heavy feeling is flowing into your shoulders, and down your arms, your upper arms, your forearms, into your hands and fingers. And now flowing back through your forearms, your upper arms, into your shoulders and into your neck. Flowing over your face, into your eyes, over your eyebrows, over your forehead, over the top of your head, down the back of your head and down the back of your neck.

ROUTINE E

And a new heaviness is starting now at the top of your head. Twice as heavy as before. Twice as heavy. Imag- ine a heavy weight on the very top of your head, soft and relaxed and heavy. Feel the heavy relaxation flow-ing down into your face and eyes now, down through your neck, your shoulders, flowing down through your chest, your waist, your hips, your thighs, your knees, into your calves, your ankles, your feet and toes. Deeply relaxed, loose and limp, and comfortable from the top of your head to the very tip of your toes.

ROUTINE F

I want you to imagine now that you are looking at a blackboard. On the blackboard imagine a circle. Into the circle we are going to place the letters of the alpha-bet in reverse order, and with each letter after you place it into the circle, you will erase it then from inside the circle and allow yourself to relax more and more deeply.

Picture the blackboard now. Picture the circle. Into the circle put the letter Z. Now erase the Z from inside the circle, and go deeper. Put Y into the circle, and erase it and go deeper. X, and erase it and go deeper still. W, and erase it. V, and erase it. U, and erase it. T, and erase it. S, and erase it. R, and erase it. Q, and erase it. P, and erase it. O, and erase it. N, and erase it. M, and erase it. L, and erase it. K, and erase it. J, and erase it. I, and erase it. H, and erase it. G, and erase it. F, and erase it. E, and erase it. D, and erase it. C, and erase it. B, and erase it. A, and erase it. Now erase the circle and forget about the blackboard. Just go on relaxing more and more deeply. Feel yourself sink into the chair, mind and body drifting deeper and deeper into relaxation, deeper with each breath.

Routine G

I want you to imagine now that you are looking at a clear, blue summer sky. And in the sky, a sky-writing airplane is writing your first name in fluffy, white cloud-like letters. See your name floating fluffy, white, and cloud-like in a clear, blue sky. Now let your name just dissolve away. Let the winds just blow your name away into the blue. Forget about your name. Forget you even have a name. Names are not important. Just go on listening to my voice and allowing yourself to relax more deeply.

Routine H

I want you to imagine now that I am placing on each of your knees a heavy bag of sand. Feel the sand pressing down on your knees. Your knees are growing heavier and more relaxed. In the sand is a very powerful numbing ingredient and the numbness is flowing down into your knees now. Your knees are growing numb and more numb under the sand. And the heavy, numb feeling is flowing down into your calves, into your ankles, into your feet and toes. Everything below your knees is numb and more numb from the sand. And now the heavy, numb feeling is going up into your thighs, flowing into your hips, through your waist, and into your chest. It flows into your shoulders, and they grow numb and heavy. It flows down your arms, your upper arms, your forearms, into your hands and fingers. Flowing back now through your forearms, your upper arms, your shoulders, and into your neck.

Over your face, your eyes. Flowing up to your eyebrows, your forehead, over the top of your head, down the back of your head, and down the back of your neck.

ROUTINE J

As you go on floating, drifting smoothly and gently, more and more deeply relaxed with each breath, I want you to focus your attention on the very tip of your nose. Keep your attention focused gently and lazily on the tip of your nose until you reach a point where your entire attention is on the sound of my voice. And when you reach that point, you can forget about your nose and just go on listening to my voice and allowing yourself to relax more and more deeply. As you keep your attention gently focused on the tip of your nose, I want you to imagine now that I am placing on your tongue, in your mouth, a small bite of chocolate candy. You don't swallow it; it just sits there on your tongue. Notice the bitter taste of the chocolate. It is bitter and it is growing more bitter and more bitter as it just sits here, melting on your tongue. It is so bitter that you can hardly keep it in your mouth. It tastes terrible. From now on you will be completely free from any desire for chocolate or candy or sweet foods of any kind. You will be completely free from that desire, completely free from now on. I am taking the bitter chocolate from your mouth now. Your mouth feels clean now, all fresh and clean. You are glad that that ugly taste is gone from your tongue.

ROUTINE K-1 (use only with female subjects)

I want you to imagine yourself. See yourself as you really want to be, the real you. Alive and vibrant, in full control, serene and lovely. This is you. This is the real you. This is the woman you can really come to be. At this moment you are making yourself a promise. Not a promise to me...a promise to yourself...a commitment to become the real you. This commitment will be with you, stronger every day. From now on, every day you will become more and more completely the lovely woman you want to be. You will be relaxed and serene no matter what is going on around you. And anything that does happen, you can handle it in a relaxed and sensible manner. And you will feel so good, you will have all the energy in the world every single day. And it will be very easy for you to stay on your diet strictly every day. No matter where you are, no matter what you are doing.

ROUTINE K-2 (use only with male subjects)

I want you to imagine yourself. See yourself as you really want to be, the real you. Confident and energetic, in full control, healthy and trim. This is you. This is the real you. This is the man you can really come to be. At this moment you are making yourself a promise. Not a promise to me...a promise to yourself...a commitment to become the real you. This commitment will be with you, stronger every day. From now on, every day you will become more and more completely the trim, handsome man you want to be.

You will be relaxed and calm no matter what is going on around you. And anything that does happen, you can handle it in a relaxed and sensible manner. And you will feel very good, you will have all the energy in the world every single day. And it will be very easy for you to stay on your diet strictly every day. No matter where you are, no matter what you are doing.

ROUTINE L

In the morning you will have a small serving of protein, a small serving of fruit or juice, and one piece of toast served without butter. For lunch you will have one small serving of protein and a small serving of fresh fruit or vegetable. For dinner you will have a small dinner salad with a very light dressing, a small serving of protein and one-half cup cooked vegetable served without butter or margarine.

ROUTINE M

You will always eat very slowly, and when you have eaten just a little of the proper sensible foods, you will feel full, completely full and satisfied on just a little bit of the right food. That is all your body needs right now. That is all you will want. You will have no desire at all for sweets or starches or rich greasy foods. The longer you stay on your diet, the easier it will be and your weight will just melt away. All those extra pounds will just disappear so fast and so easy. Every day you will be smaller and lighter and prettier, and you will feel better and better every day. And you will also practice faithfully the little exercise in self-hypnosis that we are going to do together now.

(Where the word "prettier" is used, you may find it more appropriate to use "attractive." If the subject is a man, use "handsome.")

Routine N

In a moment, I am going to ask you to open your eyes and look at a spot I am going to hold before you. You will not awaken when you open your eyes. You will not awaken. You will go even deeper into relaxation. Open your eyes now and look at the spot I am holding before you and take a deep, full breath.

(As you tell the subject to open her eyes, hold up a card that has a large, bright red spot on it for her to direct her attention to. A handy size for this card is 6 x 6 inches, preferably white card stock on which is drawn as large a circle as you can get on the card. The circle should be colored bright red. Hold the card at her eye level about 4 feet in front of her.)

Deep and full. Now close your eyes, let the breath out and think 5...5...5...and go deeper. Again now, a deep, easy breath and think 4...4...4...and let it out. Again a deep breath, deep and full, think 3...3...3... and let it out. More and more deeply relaxed. Take in a deep breath and think 2...2...2...and let it out. Once more a deep breath, let it out and think 1...1...let it all go now...1.

Imagine now a heavy, deep force of relaxation just behind your eyelids. Feel this deep, relaxing force flowing down from your eyelids. Down through your face and neck, down through your shoulders and chest, your waist, your hips, down through your thighs, your knees, your calves, your ankles, your feet and toes.

ROUTINE O

In a moment, I am going to count backward from 10 to 1. I want you to count with me silently to yourself. Think each number as I say it, and allow each number to take you deeper. 10...9...8...7...6...5...4...3...2...1. You are now very deeply relaxed. You can give yourself the following suggestions. Say the words to yourself with me as I say them: I will always be relaxed and calm. I will not want anything to eat until dinner time.

(In place of "dinner time," substitute whatever is appropriate. It may be "until lunch time" or "until tomorrow," or whatever.)

Now picture the spot that you looked at at the beginning of this exercise. Imagine the spot floating in, traveling together with your suggestions. Traveling all the way to the back of your head, all the way to the back. When you have your spot and your suggestions together at the back of your head, erase it, forget about the spot, forget about the suggestions, just let it all disappear. Allow yourself to relax.

ROUTINE P

Between now and the next time I see you, you will practice this self-hypnosis exercise faithfully at least three times every single day, even if you think you don't need it. It makes you feel just wonderful. And each time you go through this routine in self-hypnosis you will relax completely. You will go just as deep as you are now. Just as you are now, and the suggestions that you give yourself will go deeper and deeper into your mind. By practicing your self-hypnosis faithfully every day, you will have perfect control over your own appetite. You can dissolve away any hunger. You can dissolve away any tension, any craving for food or drink you shouldn't have. Every day your weight will keep on going down and you will keep on looking better and better, and you will keep on feeling good every single day.

ROUTINE Q

The next time I see you, or whenever you hear my voice on tape, you will allow yourself to relax even more completely than you are now. And the suggestions I have given you will keep on going deeper and deeper and deeper into your mind.

In a few moments when you awaken yourself, you will feel very very relaxed, and you will be completely refreshed, alive, alert, full of energy, full of confidence. You will feel simply marvelous. All you have to do to awaken is to count with me from 1 up to 5 and at the count of 5, open your eyes, feeling relaxed, refreshed,

*alert, in very high spirits. Feeling very good indeed.
1...2...3...4...5.*

After the bring-out, ask the subject how she feels.
Answer any questions she may have.

Have two pre-typed sheets of paper to give her to
keep. These are necessary for her diet control and for
practicing her self-hypnosis. One sheet has her recommended diet on it. The other sheet has her self-
hypnosis routine on it.

Sample Diet Program

Breakfast
Small serving of protein (2–3 oz.)
Small serving of juice or fruit (4 oz.)
One piece of unbuttered toast
Lunch
Small serving of protein (3–4 oz.)
Small serving of fresh fruit or vegetable
Dinner
Small serving of protein (4–5 oz.)
Small salad with light dressing
1/2 cup cooked vegetable served without butter
    or margarine
Diet drinks, except colas unless they are
    decaffeinated
Decaffeinated coffee
No gravies or sauces.
Approximately 800 to 1,000 calories per day.

The sample diet is not to be taken literally as the
diet to suggest to everyone; it is just an illustration.

Not everyone should be put on a 1,000-calories-per-day diet. Don't play doctor or nutritionist unless you actually are one. Work with your client to achieve a healthy diet. If the client has medical problems or is taking medication, you may need to have the client consult with her physician concerning any diet recommendations. Even though you have pre-printed diet sheets of this sample diet, be prepared to pencil-in changes to customize it for an appropriate diet when you discuss it with the client.

Many times, you need only focus on one dietary problem (such as eating too much candy, eating two or three portions when one would be sufficient, or drinking too much beer). In these cases you don't need to have a total dietary plan. Just create a distaste for the chocolate, beer, or whatever. The case example at the end of this chapter shows how to deal with this sort of problem.

Self-Hypnosis Instructions

Stretch! Then sit in a comfortable position.

Focus your attention on a spot, and as you do, mentally say the number 5 three times as you exhale. Then close your eyes.

Take another deep breath, and as you exhale, mentally say the number 4 three times. As you say the number 4, picture it at the same time.

Take another deep breath and do the same thing with numbers 3, 2, and 1 consecutively.

Now, imagine a relaxation force emanating from your eyes and flowing out all over your body like a warm blanket of soothing, warm, gentle air going all the way down to your toes.

Then count backward from ten to one.

After reaching the number 1, give yourself these suggestions:

I will always be relaxed and calm.

I will not want anything to eat until dinner.

Then picture the same spot in your mind that you looked at originally. Imagine this spot moving all the way to the back of your head taking the suggestion with it. Then forget the suggestion, so that your inner mind will absorb it.

Then count from 1 to 5 and awaken and feel the effect of the suggestions.

POST-SESSION WRAP-UP

Give your client sufficient time to read the diet program and the self-hypnosis instruction sheet. Answer any questions that she may have.

You need to be fairly well informed concerning diet. Keep a good nutrition book on hand for reference if necessary. Many people don't know what a protein food is, so you need to be prepared to explain and give examples.

Read the self-hypnosis instructions out loud with your client, explaining each instruction as you go. Reaffirm that she was given these instructions under hypnosis and was given the post-hypnotic suggestion that it would work just as well for her as when you perform the hypnosis.

The most important thing the subject should understand is that she *must* practice her self-hypnosis daily. There are two reasons for this.

First, she is training her mind to follow a different course than in the past. The mind prefers to do what it has always done, i.e., follow the same path. Therefore, consistent and diligent retraining is necessary. Your mind isn't going to believe you really want to change if you take a willy-nilly approach to your practice of self-hypnosis. Your mind believes you really want to overeat and be fat because that is what you have been practicing and telling it for years. Now, you want to reverse that detrimental programming. To reverse it, you must hammer into your subconscious every day what you really want until your mind is convinced of your desire for a new reality; then your mind will create this new reality...more temperate eating habits, loss of excess weight...feeling better ...looking better. Fortunately, self-hypnosis doesn't take years to achieve the re-programming. Hypnosis works quickly, sometimes instantly, most often within days or several weeks, and occasionally over several months for really stubborn problems. But you must keep at it until you have successfully achieved the re-programming.

Second, hypnotic suggestion is not permanent. If it were, it would only be necessary to have one hypnosis session and give one set of suggestions per problem and then everything would be all right—but it doesn't work that way. The length of time a hypnotic suggestion lasts effectively varies widely depending on the individual's response to hypnosis. I have seen some people who wouldn't respond to hypnotic suggestion more than a few hours to a day without the need for being reinforced with another hypnosis session. Some remain responsive for one or two weeks. A rare few, even longer than two weeks. This is why the subject needs to reinforce herself every day with the self-hypnosis until the desired results are achieved.

CASE EXAMPLE FOR DIET CONTROL

An overweight woman came to me for diet control. Her problem was that she was a compulsive popcorn eater. She bought her popcorn in 100-pound bags. She ate it morning, noon, and night and in between times, and the popcorn was always soaked to the point of dripping with real butter and loaded with salt. Then, of course, there were cases of nondiet soda pop to quench her thirst. I knew that the butter, salt, and soda pop were far more detrimental to her than the popcorn, but popcorn was the vehicle. Without the popcorn she wouldn't be consuming all those other things. So I decided to make popcorn undesirable to her.

Before hypnotizing her, I tried to find out what she didn't like. She loved everything.

"Isn't there something in life you find repulsive?" I asked in desperation.

"Well, yes," she replied. "Wet chicken feathers make me ill. I can't stand the smell. My father used to make me kill and pluck chickens against my will."

There I had my mechanism…wet chicken feathers. When I had her into routine J and I got to the part where she puts something to eat in her mouth, I said, "There is a large bowl of popcorn in front of you. The popcorn has been soaked in wet chicken feathers. The popcorn smells like wet chicken feathers. The popcorn tastes like wet chicken feathers. Now, pick up a kernel of popcorn and put it into your mouth and taste it."

She immediately began to gag and retch. I thought she was going to vomit.

After she left my office she went home and made a batch of popcorn out of habit. This time she did vomit. She tried daily to make popcorn but got nauseous just trying to make it. By the time she came back for session 3, she had stopped trying to make popcorn...she had kicked the habit and was losing excess weight. Of course, without the popcorn, she stopped drinking soda pop and eating large amounts of butter and salt.

By session 6 she had lost almost 20 pounds and was looking and feeling good. I had her add more fruit and vegetables to her diet. She was no longer a popcornaholic.

The lesson to be learned here is to find out what tastes or smells are especially offensive to your subject. Use those tastes and smells to remove the desire for the offending eating habit. Most often, the dietary habit that is causing the problem is eating sweets such as chocolate or pastries. If your subject eats five pounds of chocolate a day and hates the taste of liver, have her visualize getting some chocolate from the refrigerator where it has been lying next to five pounds of unwrapped wet liver. The liver taste and smell has impregnated all the chocolate...you get the idea.

CHAPTER 4

Hypnosis Session 3

The purpose of this session is to reinforce the hypnosis and suggestions previously given, increase the depth of hypnosis so that suggestions will be programmed in at another level of mind, and reinforce the subject's own self-hypnosis.

Before starting the induction, talk with the client about her experience with self-hypnosis since you last saw her. Has she been practicing her self-hypnosis faithfully every day? If not, why? Has she been following her diet faithfully? If not, why? Has she fairly well mastered the self-hypnosis or is she having some difficulties?

If she has been having difficulty with the self-hypnosis, go over the procedure with her again. Demonstrate on yourself just how to do it, speaking your thoughts out loud so she can observe and follow.

If she is having difficulty relaxing or concentrating, reassure her that this will disappear with practice. Tell her that many people experience this difficulty and she should not be concerned.

A frequent complaint is, "I keep forgetting what I am supposed to do in my self-hypnosis procedure." Tell her that is why you wrote down the procedure, and that it is all right to open her eyes and read it. Very quickly she will learn it from memory. Her first concern is to learn the procedure and become comfortable with it and not be concerned about results. The results will occur automatically when she learns and practices diligently.

Be sure to emphasize that she can change the suggestion portion of her self-hypnosis routine to suit any purpose she has in mind. She can have only one suggestion if she wants, or she can have many. Recommend, however, that she treat only one purpose or problem at any one time. For example, she shouldn't work on quitting smoking at the same time she is working on diet control. Handle the problems separately. The self-hypnosis routine is hers for life, so encourage her to develop the habit of using it daily for self-enrichment.

At this point in the program, the subject may not be practicing her self-hypnosis regularly. This is because her recalcitrant mind is fighting change; the mind prefers to follow the same old path rather than a new one. The subject will rationalize all sorts of reasons for not being able to perform the self-hypnosis.

There are two common reasons for not practicing self-hypnosis faithfully every day. The first one is: "I don't have, or cannot find, a spot to look at for beginning the self-hypnosis." Do not scold the subject for saying something this ridiculous. Remember, the subject's mind is fighting her and at the same time she is trying to understand and develop a new skill and a new lifestyle.

Calmly explain that the spot can be anything in her line of vision, including a doorknob, a flower on a curtain, a dirt spot on the wall, the point in the corner where the walls and ceiling meet, an electrical outlet, an upholstery button on the sofa, a burning candle flame, and an electric light bulb. It is impossible to be in a place where there is nothing in your line of vision on which to fix your gaze.

The second reason for not practicing self-hypnosis is: "I don't have time. I am never alone. I work in an office from 8 to 5 with people all around. Then I go home to my family where there are again demands on my time. I don't have a minute to myself." This is a common situation. It *is* often difficult to be alone for five minutes, three times a day, to practice your self-hypnosis.

My response to this reason goes something like this:

"Do you go to the bathroom at all during the day?" I ask.

"Of course."

"Do you take anyone with you when you go to the bathroom?"

"Of course not!"

"Then every time you sit on the toilet, use the time to perform your self-hypnosis routine."

"I didn't know it could be done sitting on the toilet," is the usual response.

"Of course you can. You can also do self-hypnosis in the bathtub while bathing. There is no limit."

I go on to explain that self-hypnosis can be practiced anywhere anytime successfully. In fact, when you really become good at it, you can do it with your eyes open with people and distractions all around. When you reach this point you will really have mastered a powerful tool that you can use instantly for virtually anything.

(You are probably getting the impression that the potential for using your altered state of consciousness goes far beyond the scope of anything covered in this book—that is a correct impression. This book is just the beginning. Your mind, your thoughts have a very real potential that far transcends diet control. For now, master the things covered in this book. When you do, the next stage of your development will automatically open up to you and you will know what to do.)

Occasionally, you will encounter a client who is unwilling to make any good faith attempt to practice the self-hypnosis or follow the diet. This person has a vast number of reasons and counter reasons for not doing so. No matter what you say or explain, her reply is, "Yes, but..." When I encounter a completely non-cooperative client such as this, I say something like: "Well, if you want to pay me good money for my services and then not cooperate with those services, that certainly is your privilege. Just be aware that you will have zero results for your time and money. I do not enjoy taking money when the client is not trying to do her part. Therefore, if this continues I will probably ask you to discontinue the sessions and save your money. Think about it. The choice is yours. Now let's proceed with today's session." I have only had to say this sort of thing twice in all my years of practice.

Both times the clients stopped playing games and started cooperating with ultimately satisfactory results.

SESSION 3 consists of 14 routines in the following sequence: A, B, C, D, E, F, I, G, H, R, L, S, T, Q.

Routines A and B are found in chapter 2. Routines C, D, E, F, G, H, L, and Q are found in chapter 3. Notice that the sequence is slightly different than in session 2.

ROUTINE I

As you breathe in, imagine that you are breathing in a pure, clean, odorless anesthesia. This anesthesia is flowing all throughout your body now, a warm, numb, tingling feeling. And the more you breathe in the more you want to breathe in, and you allow your breathing to become even deeper now, bringing in more and more of this peaceful, relaxed, tranquil feeling. From now on until the end of the session, with each breath you will allow yourself to relax more and more completely.

ROUTINE R-1 (use only with female subjects)

As you go on floating, drifting smoothly and gently more and more deeply relaxed with each breath, focus your attention on the tip of your nose. Keep your attention now focused gently and lazily on the tip of your nose until you reach a point where your entire attention is on the sound of my voice. When you reach that point you can forget about the tip of your nose and just go on listening to my voice and allowing yourself to relax more and more deeply. As you keep your attention gently focused on the tip of your nose, I want you to imagine for a minute. Imagine yourself as you really want to be, slender and pretty, looking so good and feeling so fine, so full of energy and vitality, wearing the gorgeous clothes that look so good on your slender, beautiful body. This is you. This is the lovely woman you are now becoming. Every day from now on you will be more and more completely the woman you really want to be. You will be relaxed and calm no matter what is going on around you, and anything that does happen you can handle in a relaxed and sensible manner. And you will feel so good. You will have all the energy you can use every day, and you will find it very easy to stay on your diet strictly every day, no matter where you are and no matter what you are doing.

ROUTINE R-2 (use only with male subjects)

As you go on floating, drifting smoothly and gently more and more deeply relaxed with each breath, focus your attention on the tip of your nose. Keep your attention now focused gently and lazily on the tip of your nose until you reach a point where your entire attention is on the sound of my voice. When you reach that point you can forget about the tip of your nose and just go on listening to my voice and allowing yourself to relax more and more deeply. As you keep your attention gently focused on the tip of your nose, I want you to imagine for a minute. Imagine yourself as you really want to be, trim and healthy, looking handsome

*and virile, full of confidence, energy and vitality, wear-
ing well-fitting clothes that look so good on your proportioned, firm, trim body. This is you. This is the
handsome, virile man you are now becoming. Every
day from now on you will be more and more completely the man you really want to be. You will be relaxed
and calm no matter what is going on around you, and
anything that does happen you can handle it in a
relaxed and sensible manner. And you will feel so
good. You will have all the energy you can use every
day, and you will find it very easy to stay on your diet
strictly every day, no matter where you are and no
matter what you are doing.*

ROUTINE S

*You will always eat very slowly, and when you have
eaten just a little bit of the proper, sensible foods you
will feel full, stuffed on just a little bit of the right
foods. That is all your body needs now, and that is all
you will want. You will have no desire at all to nibble
or snack in between meals or after dinner. You will
have no desire for sweets or starches or rich greasy
foods of any kind. And the longer you stay on your
diet, the easier it will be. For you are now beginning to
form the habit of eating correctly for your own body.
And as your body responds to this habit, as your stomach keeps on shrinking a little bit every day, you will
feel comfortable with less and less food, and your
weight will keep on going down even faster than
before. So fast, so smooth, and so easy. Every day you*

will keep on getting smaller and lighter and prettier, and you will feel simply marvelous every single day.

(Where the word "prettier" is used, you may find it more appropriate to use "attractive." If the subject is a man, use "handsome.")

ROUTINE T

You will continue to practice the self-hypnosis exercise faithfully as often as you can every single day, and each time you go through the routine in self-hypnosis you will relax completely. You will go just as deep as you are now, and whatever suggestions you give yourself will be stronger and go deeper all the time. By continuing to practice your self-hypnosis faithfully every day, you will have perfect control over your own appetite. You can dissolve away any hunger. You can dissolve away any tension, any craving for food or drink you should not have, any fear or anger or unnecessary pain. For you are in control now, and whatever you set your mind to do, you can and will do it. You will be completely successful and you will enjoy your success. You will enjoy looking better and feeling better every single day.

CHAPTER 5

Hypnosis Session 4

Session 4 is probably the most powerful and valuable of all six hypnosis sessions covered in this book. In this session, you develop a mechanism to enable the subject to vastly improve her self-image and deal with her problems. The mechanism is the creation of a personal, private room that the subject can always go to for problem solving.

As with other sessions, start this one by talking with the subject to find out how she is progressing with her self-hypnosis and her diet. Help her with any problems she may have encountered, then proceed with the induction.

SESSION 4 consists of 14 routines in the following sequence: A, B, C, D, E, F, I, G, U, V, W, X, Y, Q.

Routines A and B are found in chapter 2. Routines C, D, E, F, G, and Q are found in chapter 3. Routine I is found in chapter 4.

ROUTINE U

This routine is one of the most powerful and useful tools for hypnosis and self-hypnosis. It creates a

personal place—a private room or private temple—
where scientific re-programming is done. Here, the
routine is used within the context of the diet control
program. The use of this routine for self-hypnosis is
found in chapter 13.

*I want you to imagine now that you are standing
on the top step of a heavy wooden staircase. Feel the
carpet under your feet. The carpet can be any kind and
color you wish...create it. Now extend your hand out
and touch the railing. Feel the smooth polished wood
of the railing under your hand. You are standing just
ten steps up from the floor below. The stairs are curving very smoothly down to the floor below. In a
moment we will walk down the stairs. With each step
down you will allow yourself to relax even more
deeply. By the time you reach the floor below you will
be deeper than you have ever gone before. Take a step
down now, down to the ninth step smoothly and easily.
Feel yourself going deeper. Now down to 8, deeper still.
Now down to 7...6...5...4...3...2...1. Now you are
standing on the floor below. There is a door in front of
you. Reach out and open the door. And from the room
beyond the door a flood of light comes streaming out
through the open doorway. Walk into the room, into
the light through the open door. You are inside the
room now, look around you. This is your room, and it
can be anything you want it to be. Any size, any shape,
any colors. You can have anything in this room that
you want. You can add things, remove things,
rearrange things. You can have any kind of furniture,
fixtures, paintings, windows, carpets, or whatever
you want because this is your place...your very own*

*private inner place and you are free here. Free to cre-
ate, free to be who you are. Free to do whatever you
will, and the light that shines in this room is your
light. Feel the light all around you, shining on the
beautiful things in your room. Shining on you; feel the
energy in the light. Let the light flow all through your
body now. Going in through every pore in your skin.
Filling you completely. Pushing away all doubt. Pushing out all fear and tension. You are filled with the
light. You are clear and radiant, glowing with the
shining light in your room.*

ROUTINE V-1 (use only with female subjects)

*While you are standing in the light in your room, I
want you to build an image. An image of yourself as
you really want to be. Not as someone else wants you
to be, but as you really want yourself to be. See your
image standing in front of you in the light. Your image
is slender, beautiful, serene and free, wearing all those
gorgeous clothes that look so fine on your beautiful
body. This is you. This is the real you. This is the
woman you are now becoming. Walk closer to your
image now. Walk closer. Now walk into the image. Let
it blend into your very body. Your own best self, a living part of you now. Stronger every day.*

ROUTINE V-2 (use only with male subjects)

*While you are standing in the light in your room, I
want you to build an image. An image of yourself as
you really want to be. Not as someone else wants you*

to be, but as you really want yourself to be. See your image standing in front of you in the light. Your image is trim, healthy, handsome, calm and free, wearing well-fitting clothes that look so fine on your nicely proportioned body. This is you. This is the real you. This is the man you are now becoming. Walk closer to your image now. Walk closer. Now walk into the image. Let it blend into your very body. Your own best self, a living part of you now. Stronger every day.

Routine W

From now on every day you will be more and more completely the woman you really want to be. You will be relaxed and calm. And no matter what is going on around you, you can handle it in a relaxed and sensible manner. And you will feel so good. You will have all the energy you can use every single day. And it will be so easy to stay on your diet strictly every day no matter where you are.

(For a male subject, replace "woman" with "man.")

Routine X

You will always eat very slowly, and when you have eaten just a little bit of the proper, sensible foods you will feel full, stuffed on just a little bit of the right foods. That is all your body needs now, and that is all you will want. You will have no desire at all to nibble or snack in between meals or after dinner. You will have no desire at all for sweets or starches or rich

*greasy foods of any kind. All that is in the past for you
now. Your body does not need that, and you do not
even want it. For you are now forming the habit of eating correctly for your body. And your body is adjusting
to this habit more and more completely every day. As
your stomach continues to shrink a little bit every day,
you will feel full and comfortable on less and less food.
And your weight will keep on going down, even faster
than before, so fast and easy. Every day you will keep
on getting smaller and lighter and more pretty. And
you will feel simply marvelous every day.*

(Where the word "pretty" is used, you may find it more
appropriate to use "attractive." If the subject is a man,
use "handsome.")

ROUTINE Y

*You will continue to practice your self-hypnosis exer-
cise faithfully as often as you can every single day.
And each time you go through your little routine in
self-hypnosis you will relax completely. And very, very
swiftly. Within just a few seconds you will go just as
deep as you are now. Even deeper. And whatever suggestions you give to yourself will be stronger and deeper all the time. For you are in control now. Whatever
you choose to do, you can do. Whatever you set your
mind to achieve, you can and will achieve. You will be
completely successful, and you will enjoy your success.
And you will enjoy becoming more and more attractive
every day. You will enjoy feeling beautiful, more and
more your real self every day.*

CHAPTER 6

Hypnosis Sessions 5 and 6

SESSION 5

Session 5 is strictly a reinforcement session; all of its routines have been given in previous chapters. Session 5 is nearly identical to session 4; session 4 had one additional routine (V) that is only presented once to a given subject.

This is the session I usually record on cassette tape because it is an exceptionally powerful and effective session. I give the tape to the subject to keep.

During your initial dialog with the subject, remind her that the room she created in session 4 (and which is reinforced in session 5) is an especially important tool. She can return to this room via her self-hypnosis anytime she wants for any good purpose she wants. In this room, she can create her own reality for a better and more enriching life. She is in direct contact with her own higher mind in this room, so she will be able to get results more effectively.

SESSION 5 consists of 13 routines in the following sequence: A, B, C, D, E, F, I, G, U, W, X, Y, Q.

Routines A and B are found in chapter 2; routines C, D, E, F, G, and Q are found in chapter 3; routine I is found in chapter 4; routines U, W, X, and Y are found in chapter 5.

Session 6

Session 6 is also primarily a reinforcement session. Twelve of its routines have already been given in previous chapters. The new routine, Z, which I call the Mountain Trip, is a very important one. This routine allows the subject to expand her creativity and begin to explore her own higher mind and the vast resource of higher intelligence available to her. I have seen some beautiful, powerful, mind-blowing experiences occur during the experiencing of this routine.

SESSION 6 consists of 13 routines in the following sequence: A, B, C, D, E, F, I, G, Z, W, X, Y, Q.

Routines A and B are found in chapter 2; routines C, D, E, F, G, and Q are found in chapter 3; routine I is found in chapter 4; routines W, X, and Y are found in chapter 5.

Routine Z: Mountain Trip

Find yourself lying on a soft, green meadow of grass with the bright sun overhead. Notice the flowers around your head. The gentle breeze gently blows across your body. Notice the grass and flowers spring up to about a foot above your head. See how the breeze gently blows the blades of grass back and forth. Smell the fragrance of the flowers.

Now stand up and look to the north. See a majestic mountain at the end of this meadow. Let's take a trip up that mountain. There is a stream on the right of you. Bend down and notice the cool water. Take a drink of this absolutely pure clean cool refreshing water. Listen to the rush of the small rapids on this bubbly brook.

Since the stream seems to come from the mountain, let's follow it. Now we come upon a pond that is at the head of this stream. Notice how warm the water is here. Since at this level of mind we are all expert swimmers, lets go for a swim. Feel the warm sun. Feel the warm water surrounding your body as you quietly move through the water.

It is now time for us to continue up the mountain. As we climb, listen to the birds chirping. Smell the pine trees. Look at the rocks on the bank to our left. Once in awhile, we can see the valley and our meadow on the right between the trees. We are halfway up the mountain now. Lets stop to rest on the rock to our right. Our meadow is in full view from here. It is now time to continue up to the top of the mountain. Listen to the squirrels chatter in the trees above.

The breeze is blowing the smell of the small cedar trees to us as we near the top. We are on the top now. We can see a deep canyon on the other side. There is a sign on the top of our mountain. It says, "Yell the questions you most want answered into the canyon below, and see the answer written in the sky above. So yell *your question now...and see the answer in the sky above. Now ask another question. See the answer in the sky above.*

Now it is time for us to return to our meadow. See the sun starting to set on the hills to the left. If we hurry, we can be off our mountain before it gets dark. Halfway down the mountain now, and we stop to rest on our rock again. We can watch the beginning of the sunset. Start on down the mountain again. Hear the chirping of the small night animals. Passing our pond, we see the reflection of the sunset in its mirror surface. Our small stream is cool and refreshing as we pass along its side. Now we are back to our meadow. Lie down again in the tall grass. Smell again the flowers' fragrance. Notice the grass and flowers return to their original height as our meadow and mountain now gently fade from view.

PART II

Regression and
Self-Regression

CHAPTER 7

Regression

Regression is a trip in time to an earlier period—either an earlier period in this current life or a past life. Hypnosis is an excellent tool for making this trip backward.

You should not attempt to regress someone until you have become a reasonably experienced hypnotist. This is because an inexperienced operator can cause the regression to be a traumatic and unpleasant experience for the subject. For example, suppose you regressed a person to a past life just at the moment he or she was being beheaded? That could be a terrifying moment for your subject because it is a real experience. The regression routine outlined below shows how to prevent and/or handle such events in a subject's past life.

For certain kinds of situations, usually in the treatment of various mental or emotional disorders, it may be necessary or desirable to have the subject experience the pain, torment, fright, or whatever. This is strictly the domain of a trained psychiatrist, psychologist, or medical doctor. If you are not one of these three disciplines, stay 100 percent away from using regression in this manner.

This chapter deals with regression in a safe way for your subject. (Self-regression, which is handled a bit differently, is covered in complete detail in chapter 8.)

I only regress persons who have been previously hypnotized either by me or someone else. I want my regression subject to be already familiar with hypnosis. (This is just my personal modus operandi; I don't know that it is necessary. As you have probably guessed by now, I am a "play it safe" hypnotist. I do not take any chances or risks with my subjects. I recommend you do likewise. I have had to correct problems created by inept hypnotists, and it angers me that some operators are so careless and insensitive. This is part of the reason for my writing this book: to teach how hypnosis can, and should, be done in a caring, safe, helpful, and professional way.)

REGRESSION CASE EXAMPLES

What are the uses of regression? Following are two examples of how I used regression.

Case 1

A thirty-five-year-old man came to me with chronic back pain. He had had this pain for as long as he could recall, and it was with him all of the time. Fortunately, he had an innate high tolerance for pain, but it still was a source of discomfort and irritability for him. He had no history of injury or illness. He had been to a number of physicians who all told him the same thing: "There is no physical cause for your pain."

They implied that he was imagining it, but he felt pain; it was real.

I regressed the man back to the time when he first experienced the pain. He was sixteen years old and was preparing to try out for the high school basketball team. The pain was so severe that he was unable to try out. His days as an athlete were finished.

Continued investigation under hypnotic regression revealed that he had been the basketball star in a small midwestern school. He was a local hero. Everyone knew him. Girls vied for his attention. Then his father's employment caused the family to move to Chicago. He enrolled in a huge high school full of top-quality athletes. Competition was fierce. His high school class alone had more students than the entire twelve grades of his previous school. Being a basketball hero in the small school carried no weight in this new school.

When tryout time came, he was fearful of failure against the formidable competition. His fear was compounded because he had done considerable bragging about his previous basketball glories.

Guess what happened? He suddenly developed a severe back pain that prevented him from competing. Now he had a reason that everyone would understand and sympathize with; one that kept him from being on the team. He now could be a knowledgeable spectator, second-guessing the coaches and players from the spectator seats, and revel in his past athletic achievements.

While still under hypnosis, I led him to understand the nature of his problem. Then I told him that his back pain belonged to a previous era and that it (the pain) was not needed in his current life experience. I told him his back pain was frozen in 1964 and that it could not leave that period. Then I slowly brought him forward in time to the present. When he opened his eyes, he was totally free of pain for the first time in his recollection. He remains free of pain today. The total time of this regression session was about one hour.

Of course, it is possible that he could create another pain (or other symptom) if he again encounters a situation that he doesn't believe he can cope with. I doubt he will, though, because he learned about the games people can play with themselves. I also spent some time counseling him about how to cope and solve problems.

Case 2

A sixteen-year-old girl was my client for weight/diet control. She was a compulsive eater but the real problem was a poor self-image. I had her on the six-session diet control program described in Part I. I saw her once a week, and my main thrust was self-image improvement. She was a superb hypnosis subject, and after just five sessions, she had lost an acceptable, healthy amount of weight, had stopped her compulsive eating, and most importantly had altered her self-image. She really liked and respected herself.

I felt that she didn't really need to return for the sixth session, and started to write her a refund check for the last session (her mother had prepaid for all six sessions). She asked me to allow her to return for the last session. Instead of the diet program, she asked if I would do past life regression on her for that final session. I agreed.

I took her through one death cycle and one birth cycle. In my regression instructions to her I also told her to go back to a previous life experience, if any, that had a direct and important relationship to her current life. She experienced episodes in several lifetimes, including the death of her husband to whom she was deeply devoted. In all of the experiences, she loved and was loved. She experienced hard work and learned the importance and satisfaction of hard work. She experienced being needed and doing a competent job.

The regression turned out to be a beautiful experience for her, and she received two unexpected bonuses. First, she came out of the regression with an even greater feeling of self-worth and a great love of life. She developed a deep understanding in those few minutes that transformed her whole perspective about life. Everything reinforced the self-image work we had achieved in the previous five sessions. Second, and here is a real kicker, she recognized the husband who had died as being the same boy to whom she was currently engaged. Although they did not look the same and had entirely different names and nationalities, her acute awareness under deep hypnosis brought her this knowledge.

The Regression Routine

Getting Ready

First, use a series of deep relaxation and visualization techniques to achieve hypnosis exactly as detailed in Part I. The specific routines and sequence are your choice, based on your own experience and preference. One example is to use routines A, B, C, D, E, F, I, G, H.

When you finish directing routine H, start into the regression routine detailed in the next section. This regression routine is a general approach; improvise your own wording to fit your needs. To direct a person to a current life regression, you will use different words than to direct to a past life regression. When you question the subject under hypnosis and carry on a dialogue, you will need to question or say whatever is appropriate. In large measure, what you ask or direct are dependent on the answers you receive from the subject.

The Routine

Now I am going to count backward from 10 to 1. Each number I say will take you to an even deeper state of relaxation. When I reach 1, you will find yourself standing on a white sand beach facing a beautiful, deep blue ocean. 10...9...8...7...6...5...4...3...2...1. You are now standing on a white sand beach facing a beautiful, deep blue ocean. The ocean is the ocean of life, and it stretches endlessly before you, and to the left, and to the right. You are standing on the sands of time. The sands of time stretch endlessly to your left and to your right. Now turn your head and look to your left. The sands of time are stretching endlessly into the future. Notice a fog bank on the beach that prevents you from currently seeing beyond it. Now turn your head and look to your right. The sands of time are stretching endlessly into the past. Notice a fog bank on the beach that prevents you from currently seeing beyond it.

In a few moments, we are going to walk down the beach to the right, into the fog bank that is currently clouding the past. You will always be able to hear my voice and follow my instructions. When I ask you questions, you will be able to answer me verbally out loud.

Now I want you to turn to your right and walk down the sands of time into the past. Into the fog bank. The fog bank now surrounds you completely. It is cool, refreshing, and comfortable. You may stop walking now. Just stand in the fog bank. In a few moments, I will count backward from 10 to 1, and each number I say will take you further and further back in time as the fog bank begins to dissolve. When I reach 1, the fog bank will be completely dissolved and you will find yourself in a previous life experience, if there were any, that had a direct and important relationship to your current life. Any experiences you may have you will view as though you are watching a movie. You will have complete awareness of all detail, of your thoughts and emotions, of who you are, where you are, what you are doing. Just as in a movie, you will be aware of joy or pain, sorrow or love, awareness of all feeling and emotion, but you will not physically experience it. You will be able to observe it and tell me about it. Anytime I say the word "RELAX," whatever experience you are having at the time will immediately disappear and you will take a deep breath and settle into peaceful relaxation while listening to the sound of my voice and following my directions.

I am now going to count from 10 down to 1, and you will go progressively back in time with each count down. At the count of 1, the fog bank will be entirely dissolved and you will find yourself in a previous life experience.

10...9...8...7...6...5... 4...3...2...1. You are now in a previous life experience. Look around you. What do you see?

(Wait for response.)

Who are you?

(Wait for response.)

NOTE: At this point your dialog must be improvised. If the subject should encounter an experience that is undesirable and causes anxiety, just say "RELAX." The experience will disappear and you can direct her to another experience by saying the following: *I am now going to count from 1 to 3 and snap my fingers. At that time you will find yourself*

(Fill in your own words for whatever is appropriate such as "in another past life experience," "one year later," or "a day earlier.")

1...2...3.

(Snap fingers.)

You are now

(Fill in your own words for whatever is appropriate.)

When you are ready to bring the subject back to the current time and awaken her, say the following:

Relax and go deeper. In a few moments I am going to count from 1 up to 10. When I reach 10 you will be back to

(Say the current time, date, and year; for example, 5 P.M., July 4, 1997.)

and you will be aware of sitting comfortably in a chair with your eyes still closed. 1...2...3...4...5... 6...7...8...9...10. It is now

(Repeat the time, date, and year.)

and you are relaxing comfortably in a chair with your eyes still closed. I am now going to count from 1 to 5 and snap my fingers. At that time you will open your eyes and be wide awake and feeling fine. You will have complete recall of everything you have just experienced. 1...2...you are coming up slowly now...3...at the count of five you will open your eyes and be wide awake and feeling fine...4...5

(Snap fingers.)

Open eyes! Wide awake and feeling fine!

Analysis

With your subject, discuss as much or as little about the regression session as either of you care to. The discussion provides a great learning tool for both of you.

The wording in the regression procedure is very important. Do not be tempted to take short cuts.

Notice the symbology and visualization I use in the beginning: sands of time, ocean of life, and fog bank. Notice I said *we* are going to walk down the beach; I didn't say *you*—I want the subject to know she is not alone on this trip; it keeps me in her acute awareness no matter where she goes. That way I am always present to help her and converse with her.

Notice I emphasize that she will always be able to hear my voice and follow my instructions and converse with me. I am her security blanket.

Notice how I handled the situation so she will not feel trauma but will still be aware of it by employing the movie screen as a mechanism. I built in the key word "relax" as a device to leave an experience. This is both a safety tool and a transition tool.

To go deeper, I count down. For coming out, I count up. Notice that I first tell the subject what I am going to do: "In a moment I will count...and you will be aware...." Then I say, "I am now going to count ...and you are aware...." A subtle, but important change of wording.

I tell the subject that she will have total recall when she awakens. Strictly speaking, this is not necessary because the subject always has recall after hypnosis unless the operator tells her that she won't. I feel recall is the whole advantage of regression, so I throw that statement in just as a reinforcement. Leave that sentence out of the procedure if you wish.

Regression requires much preparation on the part of the operator. You need to think through the purpose of the regression in advance. Have the general direction of your questions clearly in mind. And be prepared to improvise on the spot for whatever direction the events take.

Do not put words in the subject's mouth or suggest to the subject what she might expect to experience. Notice that in the procedure I do not say she *will* go to a past life experience. I say, "...previous life experience, *if there were any*...." Under hypnosis, the subject will always try to please the operator. If you say to a man, "Go to a previous life experience where you were a woman," he will create such a life even if there really wasn't one. When he creates it, he will be aware that he is making it up, but he doesn't care because that is what you asked for.

Choose your words very carefully or you will likely not have a valid regression session. Do not impose your own ideas or concepts on the subject.

One final note about excursions in time. In my procedure, I said the future is to the left, and it is. Is it possible to progress in time as well as regress? Yes. I do not, however, cover this subject in this book. You probably should not fool around with progression until you are very, very experienced in all other phases of hypnosis. The mechanism, however, is there to do so.

Many other regression techniques exist that work fine. The routine outlined in this chapter is my technique. Use it, develop your own, or use some other routine that you discover in talking with other hypnotists.

CHAPTER 8

Self-Regression

This chapter provides a word-for-word procedure for using self-hypnosis to experience past life regression. The information is intended for your personal use on yourself. It is not intended for any therapeutic use, and should not be used as such. Therapeutic uses of hypnosis should always be under the guidance of a licensed medical practitioner in concert with a certified hypnotherapist.

Use of this procedure can provide many hours of enjoyment. As with all hypnosis procedures, however, there are no guarantees as to each person's success. Everyone is unique, and not everyone can be successfully self-regressed. The depth of experience you may obtain from using the information depends entirely on you. It depends on how diligent and persistent you are in your practice of self-regression, how well you respond to self-hypnosis direction, and how willing you are to allow yourself to relax and let go.

About 90 percent of the people who read this book can successfully hypnotize themselves to some extent, and 90 percent of those will have some rewarding past life experiences. The odds are that if you perform the self-regression as directed in this chapter, you will have some satisfying results.

To use hypnosis to experience past-life regression, you will record a series of four scripts. These scripts provide the procedure and instructions for creating self-regression tapes that will guide you into an altered state of consciousness that is deeply relaxing and peaceful. These tapes can enable you to successfully practice self-regression. Before we enter into an actual altered state experience of regression, however, following is information about the regression tapes and the regression experience itself.

Regression means to go back. In the case of these tapes, it means to go back in time to an earlier experience either in this current lifetime or a previous lifetime experience when you were someone else.

The reason it is possible for you to go back to previous lifetimes is because you have always existed as an intelligent energy. You always will continue to exist as an intelligent energy. Currently, you temporarily inhabit a container that you call your body. In the past you have temporarily inhabited other containers.

All experiences that ever were are now recorded indestructibly in the energies of time. And all time exists concurrently with all other time. It is only our human perception of time that makes it seem as though the past is gone. In reality the past is not gone, and it can be reached if you know how.

These tapes teach you how.

After you record the four scripts, all you need to do is to play them back, following the instructions, and enjoy the results.

About the Tapes

Tape One guides you into a deep, peaceful, altered state of consciousness experience that prepares you for your journeys into the past. Tape One does not take you into a past experience, but prepares you for Tape Two, which takes you into a past experience. Do not use any of the other tapes until you have first finished Tape One completely—it is vitally important that you use these tapes in sequence: first Tape One, then Tape Two, then Tape Three, and finally Tape Four.

Tape Two takes you into a number of regressions to past experiences in your current lifetime. It also guides you through the experience of directing yourself into a current life regression.

Tape Three takes you into a number of regressions into past life experiences. It also shows you how to direct yourself into a past life regression.

Tape Four takes you deep into an altered state of consciousness and brings you to the point of departing into the past. At that point the tape stops, and you direct yourself into whatever past experiences you choose.

After completing Tape Four, you will only need to use Tape Four in all future regressions. If you wish to refresh yourself by using the other tapes, you may do so.

The tapes have all the safeguards, guides, and protections programmed into them so you will be able to have successful, enjoyable, and educational trips into your past lives. Built in are several methods you can use to leave a particular regression whenever you want to. At no time will you ever be in a situation that you cannot handle.

These techniques for regression allow you to observe your past life experiences as though you were viewing a motion picture on a theater or TV screen. You will be fully aware of all details. You will be fully aware of all emotions, thoughts, words, and actions, but you will not physically feel any trauma.

For example, let's suppose you regressed to a lifetime when you were a soldier in the Crusades. You are in battle, and your enemy runs you through with his sword. You will not feel any pain from the sword. You will experience the entire episode much the same as if you were watching a movie. When someone in a movie gets hurt or killed, you are aware of all the detail, but you don't feel anything. The same is true with this regression technique. The only difference is that it is you, and not someone acting in a movie.

If you should regress through a previous death or through a rebirth into a new container, you will indeed experience the whole thing except for actual pain. You will be aware of the pain, but not actually feel it.

Regression using the method employed in these tapes is perfectly safe. There is no way you can be harmed, and you cannot be trapped in a particular past time. You are always in control and can always direct yourself into or out of any experience.

The Benefits of Regression

What are some of the things that you may get out of regression?

Enjoyment. It is pleasurable to explore past life experiences because they are very much a part of you.

Knowledge. The more you know about your past, the more you can understand your present. Perhaps you have a current skill that is so natural you wonder how you got it. In regression you might find that you were trained in that skill in a previous lifetime and the skill carried over into this one.

Information. You can bring back valid data from previous periods.

Explanations. There are probably people in this life that you instantly like or love, and those that you instantly do not like or despise. Through regression you may find out why.

I immediately despised a man I met in this life, and likewise he despised me. There was no rational explanation for it because we had not known each other before, and neither of us had done anything to the other. Years later in one of my past life regressions, I encountered this man. He had murdered the woman I loved, and I in turn had killed him. That explained it.

Things to Keep in Mind

Following are several important things about regression you need to know.

You will always remember your experiences after you return from the regression.

You will recognize the people in past lives who you also know in this current life. They will not look the same, have the same names, and may not even be the same sex, but you will recognize them.

You may or may not always be the same sex in past lives as you are in your current life. Even though you look different, you will always be aware that it is you.

There is no fixed period of time after a death from one life before a rebirth into another life. I have encountered cases where someone rebirthed within minutes of their death. I have had other cases where many earth years passed between a death and a rebirth, and many cases with everything in between.

When you relive a past experience it will be real—although you may think you are just making it up. Those who are new at experiencing regression think that they have made up the events. Dismiss the thought. You are not making it up. It is real and you are experiencing it as it was.

The more times you regress, the more successful you become and the more vivid and complete is the experience.

Do not be discouraged if, in the beginning, you do not have as complete or vivid an experience as you want. Keep at it. You will succeed if you persist.

RECORDING THE TAPES

You will need a cassette tape recorder and two 90-minute cassettes (45 minutes on each side). Record the script for Tape One on the first side of one cassette; record the script for Tape Two on the reverse side; record Tape Three on side one of the second cassette; record Tape Four on the reverse side. When you finish your recording, you will have a complete self-hypnosis package for past life regression.

As you read and record the scripts, speak slowly and clearly, pausing a second or so between sentences (pause longer where indicated). Use an even, monotone voice; do not record a dramatic or emotional reading. Self-hypnosis works best when you sound almost boring, because you want to bore your conscious mind so that it stops thinking, thus allowing your subconscious mind to automatically respond to the hypnosis commands.

Record all of each script except for instructions in parentheses (for example, *pause 60 seconds).* The instructions inform you to stop talking while allowing the tape to continue running. When the instruction indicates *snap,* physically snap your fingers. If you can't snap your fingers, substitute a similar sound such as slapping a ruler sharply against a tabletop. As you will see when you read the regression scripts, the snapping sound is important.

You may wish to record the script for Tape One first and listen to it. If you aren't satisfied with it, simply re-record it. When you obtain the tone and pace that works best for you, record the other tapes. With a little practice, you will succeed.

At the beginning of each session, take the phone off the hook so you won't be disturbed; sit or lie in a comfortable position; and turn on the recording and listen, following the instructions you have recorded.

PREPARATION

Tape One (recording script)

Close your eyes. Take a deep, full breath and exhale slowly. Take another deep breath and exhale. One more time a deep, full breath and hold it in. Now let it out completely and feel yourself relaxing more.

I want you to imagine now that all your tensions, all your tightness, and all your fears and worries are draining away from the top of your head. Let it drain down through your face, down through your neck, through your shoulders, through your chest, your waist, your hips, your thighs, down through your knees, your calves, your ankles, your feet and out your toes. All your tension, all your tightness, all your worries and fears are draining away now from the very tips of your toes, and you are relaxing more and more.

Focus your attention on your toes now and allow your toes to relax completely. Each toe is loose and heavy. Now let this relaxation flow into your feet, into your ankles, your calves, your knees. Feel it flowing into your thighs, into your hips, into your waist, flowing up into your chest now. Feel your breathing easier and deeper, more regular and more relaxed. Now let the deep relaxed feeling go into your shoulders, down your arms, into your upper arms, your forearms, and into your hands and fingers, and flowing back into your forearms, your upper arms, your shoulders. Flowing into your neck, over your face, your chin, your cheeks, even your ears are relaxed. Feel it flowing into your eyes and eyelids now. Your eyelids are so heavy and smooth. Flowing up into your eyebrows, over your forehead, over the top of your head, down the back of your head, and down the back of your neck.

A new heaviness is starting in your toes now. Twice as heavy as the first time. Imagine a heavy weight on each toe. Feel the heaviness deep and even more relaxed. And this heavy, deep feeling is going into your feet, your ankles, your calves, your knees, going into your thighs, your hips, into your waist. Flowing up into your chest now, relaxing your heart, relaxing your lungs, allowing your breathing to be more intense, more regular, more and more completely relaxed. Now the deep heavy feeling is flowing into your shoulders, and down your arms, your upper arms, your forearms, into your hands and fingers. And now flowing back through your forearms, your upper arms, into your shoulders and into your neck. Flowing over your face, into your eyes, over your eyebrows, over your forehead, over the top of your head, down the back of your head and down the back of your neck.

And a new heaviness is starting now at the top of your head. Twice as heavy as before. Twice as heavy. Imagine a heavy weight on the very top of your head, soft and relaxed and heavy. Feel the heavy relaxation flowing down into your face and eyes now, down through your neck, your shoulders, flowing down through your chest, your waist, your hips, your thighs, your knees, into your calves, your ankles, your feet and toes. Deeply relaxed, loose and limp, and comfortable from the top of your head to the very tip of your toes.

I want you to imagine now that you are looking at a blackboard. On the blackboard imagine a circle.

Into the circle we are going to place the letters of the alphabet in reverse order, and with each letter after you place it into the circle, you will erase it then from inside the circle and allow yourself to relax more and more deeply.

Picture the blackboard now. Picture the circle. Into the circle put the letter Z. Now erase the Z from inside the circle, and go deeper. Put Y into the circle, and erase it and go deeper. X, and erase it and go deeper still. W, and erase it. V, and erase it. U, and erase it. T, and erase it. S, and erase it. R, and erase it. Q, and erase it. P, and erase it. O, and erase it. N, and erase it. M, and erase it. L, and erase it. K, and erase it. J, and erase it. I, and erase it. H, and erase it. G, and erase it. F, and erase it. E, and erase it. D, and erase it. C, and erase it. B, and erase it. A, and erase it. Now erase the circle and forget about the blackboard. Just go on relaxing more and more deeply. Feel yourself sink into the chair, mind and body drifting deeper and deeper into relaxation, deeper with each breath.

As you breathe in, imagine that you are breathing in a pure clean, odorless anesthesia. The anesthesia is flowing all throughout your body now. It is a warm, numb, tingling feeling, and the more you breathe in, the more you want to breathe in, and you allow your breathing to become even deeper now, bringing in more and more of this peaceful, relaxing, tranquil feeling. From now on until the end of this session, you will allow yourself to relax more and more completely with each breath you take.

I want you to imagine now that you are looking at a clear, blue summer sky. And in the sky, a sky-writing airplane is writing your first name in fluffy, white cloud-like letters. See your name floating fluffy, white, and cloud-like in a clear, blue sky. Now let your name just dissolve away. Let the winds just blow your name away into the blue. Forget about your name. Forget you even have a name. Names are not important. Just go on listening to my voice and allowing yourself to relax more deeply.

I want you to imagine now that you are standing on the top step of a heavy wooden staircase. Feel the carpet under your feet. The carpet can be any kind and color you wish—create it. Now extend your hand out and touch the railing. Feel the smooth polished wood of the railing under your hand. You are standing just ten steps up from the floor below. The stairs are curving very smoothly down to the floor below. In a moment we will walk down the stairs. With each step down you will allow yourself to relax even more deeply. By the time you reach the floor below you will be deeper than you have ever gone before. Take a step down now, down to the ninth step smoothly and easily. Feel yourself going deeper. Now down to 8, deeper still. Now down to 7...6...5...4...3...2...1. Now you are standing on the floor below. There is a door in front of you. A sign on the door reads, "Doorway to the Beach of Time." Reach out and open the door. A stream of golden sunlight pours through the open door. Walk through the door into the golden sunlight.

Before you stretches a beach of gleaming white sand. Beyond the edge of the beach is an endless ocean of clear blue-green water. Walk forward on the beach until you come to the place where the dry sand meets the wet sand near the water's edge. Stand here a moment and absorb all the sights and sounds.

Notice the sea gulls in the sky above. Watch them dive for their dinner in the sea below. Listen to their chatter as they return to the sky. Notice the other birds around you. They show their appreciation for life in their smooth gliding and happy song.

Look at the majestic expanse of ocean in front of you. It stretches as far as you can see. A gentle wave comes ashore and rushes past your feet. Feel how it tugs at you as it recedes back to the ocean. This ocean is the infinite sea of never-ending life and consciousness. Wade out into the water a short distance to where the water comes to your knees. This sea, of which you are a part, contains all the power you will ever need. Feel the power coming from the ocean floor up through your feet and legs bringing with it love and zest for life. Bringing with it courage and faith. Stand there and allow this priceless gift from the sea to fill your entire body. Flowing up through your legs. Into the trunk of your body. Flowing into your neck and head. You are filled from the sea of consciousness and life. You feel vibrant with love for life and for all. A powerful peace settles over you. Courage has filled every facet of your being. You know you can handle anything in a sensible and beneficial manner. You fear nothing at all. You have no fear, and this is so. Tremendous faith races through you. There is no room for doubt, and you have no doubts. You have received faith, courage, power, and zest for life from this infinite source of goodness. Now walk back to the beach to the point where an occasional wave washes past your ankles. Bend down and write in the wet sand with your finger this message: "I Love." Now under your "I Love" message write the names of all those special people you wish to send love. Be sure to include your own name. I will stop talking for one minute while you write the names.

(Pause 60 seconds.)

If you have not yet written your own name, do so quickly now.

(Pause 5 seconds.)

Now a wave from the sea of consciousness washes up over your message and past your ankles. The wave recedes, washing the beach clean. Your love message has been carried into the sea of universal consciousness where it has become reality. Bend down and write in the wet sand once more. This time write "I forgive" followed by your own name first, and then the names of all whom you believe have wronged you in some way. I will give you one minute now to do this.

(Pause 60 seconds.)

Now at the end of your list write these words: "and all others." Now another wave from the sea of infinite consciousness washes over your message and past your ankles. When the wave retreats to the sea, it takes with it your message of forgiveness which has now become reality. You have now purged yourself of guilt, blame, and animosity. You have filled your life with love, courage, faith, and zest. You are in balance and in harmony with all. You are now ready to serve with integrity and success.

Now stand up and face the sea of life once again. Turn your head to the right and look up the beach. That is the direction of the past. There is a closed door a short distance from you in that direction. A sign on the door reads, "Doorway to the past." Now turn your head around to your left and look up the beach in that direction. That is the direction of the future. There is a closed door a short distance from you in that direction. A sign on the door reads, "Doorway to the future."

Now look back toward the sea of life and consciousness. The breeze from the ocean brings you the awareness of what you must do now. You must open the door to the past so you can enter it and go back in time to a previous period. Turn to your right now and walk to the door of the past. There is a key hanging on a nail on the door jam. Take the key into your hand and unlock the door. Put the key back onto the nail. Push the door open all the way. Beyond the door you see a thick, silver fog bank that is currently blocking your view of the past. You have opened the door to the past, and you will return here another time to learn how to walk through the door, dissolve the fog bank, and enter a previous life experience.

Now walk back up the beach toward the door to the future until you are about halfway there. You are halfway there now. It is the present moment. Turn and face the sea of life and consciousness again. Look up into the sky at the beautiful, life-giving sun. Allow the sun to come down from the sky until it is sitting on top of your head. It is coming down. It is warm and relaxing, but not burning. Lower and lower it comes until it rests gently on top of your head. Now allow the sun to flow down into your body, filling you completely with life's power and protection. A powerful shield of white light completely surrounds your body. This shield is a positive energy shield that will be with you from now on. It protects you from harmful effects of any negative experience you may encounter. Negative energies cannot penetrate this shield. This means that you can see, experience, observe, and be fully aware of all experiences whether negative or positive, but the negative ones cannot penetrate and cause you harm or difficulties. The positive energies can penetrate and benefit you. You benefit from the negative experiences by being aware of them and having knowledge of them without experiencing difficulty from them. This positive shield also allows your positive energies to go out and help others. Your positive shield holds in any negative energies that you may create yourself so you cannot harm others. Of course this means you can only have difficulties from negative energies that you yourself create. Therefore, resolve now to be careful to not create negative energies. Say the following words to yourself as I say them: "I will harbor only positive thoughts regarding myself and others. If I start to entertain negative thoughts, I will become immediately aware of it, and I will cancel the thought and replace it with a positive, constructive thought."

Now allow the sun to return to the sky, leaving behind the powerful positive shield which will envelop you from now on at all times.

Now it is time to leave the beach until the next time. Walk back toward the doorway through which you entered the beach. There is a seashell lying along your path. Pick up the seashell and put it to your ear and listen to the message from the shell. Turn and look at the sea once more and say, "Good-bye." It is time to go back through the doorway and to the stairs of life. You have the love and excitement of life drawn up from the sea within you now. Say a special thanks to those people who have been thoughtful to you as your sea fades from view. Now walk through the doorway and leave the beach. You are now at the bottom of your spiral staircase. I will now count from one to ten. With each number I say, take one step up your staircase until you reach the top.

1...2...3...4...5...6...7...8...9... 10.

You are now at the top of your staircase. In the future when you wish to enter the beach of time, all you need to do is to come to your staircase, walk down the stairs, and go through the door to the beach just as you have experienced moments ago.

On future trips to the beach of time, you will go through the door to the past and relive past life experiences.

You have just learned how to go to the beach of time and how to return. If you are in an altered state of consciousness or in a past life experience and an emergency situation should occur in your current lifetime that requires your immediate presence and awareness, your mind will immediately pull you from the regression and altered state back into your current life and conscious awareness so you can deal with the emergency situation. This important safeguard is now programmed into your mind permanently for your benefit and welfare. You will not experience any harmful or uncomfortable side effects from being pulled immediately back to current time and awareness.

The next time you hear my voice you will allow yourself to relax ten times more deeply than you are now and the suggestions I give you then will go ten times deeper into every level of your mind.

In a few moments I will awaken you. When you awaken you will feel great. Full of energy and enthusiasm. You will feel simply terrific, and you will continue to feel terrific all the rest of the day. All you need to do to awaken is to count mentally with me as I count from one to five and then open your eyes.

1...2...coming up slowly now. 3...4...5.

(Snap.)

Open eyes, wide awake, feeling fine.

(Turn off tape recorder.)

You have been guided through the procedure for altering your state of consciousness and for entering and leaving the beach of time. You have been programmed with an important safeguard in the event an emergency situation occurs while you are in an altered state of consciousness. You have been given a powerful positive energy shield to protect you from the effects of external negative influences. You have been given the post-hypnotic suggestion to go ten times deeper the next time you hear the voice.

Now you are ready to regress to a past experience. Tape Two will take you to several past experiences within this current lifetime. You may play Tape Two anytime you wish now. My recommendation is that you wait for at least an hour while you get up and move around and do something else—your body will appreciate the break. I also recommend that you do not wait more than a week before playing Tape Two. This is so you can get maximum benefit from the suggestions given you in Tape One. Hypnotic suggestions tend to weaken over a period of time.

CURRENT LIFE REGRESSION

Tape Two guides you into a deeply relaxing and peaceful altered state of consciousness. Then it guides you into a series of regressions into the past of your current life. It also gives you the opportunity to direct yourself to several past experiences in this lifetime.

When you use this tape, you will be asking yourself a number of questions, such as "Where are you?" and "How do you feel?" Answer these questions out loud. Keep a pen or pencil and writing paper handy so you can record your regression experiences after you return to the present time. If you prefer, have a blank tape on hand to put into your tape recorder so you can verbally record your experiences afterward.

Now find a comfortable position for you to sit or lie in for about thirty-five minutes.

Tape Two (recording script)

Close your eyes. Take a deep, full breath and exhale slowly. Take another deep breath and exhale. One more time a deep, full breath and hold it in. Now let it out completely and feel yourself relaxing more.

I want you to imagine now that all your tensions, all your tightness, and all your fears and worries are draining away from the top of your head. Let it drain down through your face, down through your neck, through your shoulders, through your chest, your waist, your hips, your thighs, down through your knees, your calves, your ankles, your feet and out your toes. All your tension, all your tightness, all your worries and fears are draining away now from the very tips of your toes, and you are relaxing more and more.

Focus your attention on your toes now and allow your toes to relax completely. Each toe is loose and heavy. Now let this relaxation flow into your feet, into your ankles, your calves, your knees. Feel it flowing into your thighs, into your hips, into your waist, flowing up into your chest now. Feel your breathing easier and deeper, more regular and more relaxed. Now let the deep relaxed feeling go into your shoulders, down your arms, into your upper arms, your forearms, and into your hands and fingers, and flowing back into your forearms, your upper arms, your shoulders. Flowing into your neck, over your face, your chin, your cheeks, even your ears are relaxed. Feel it flowing into your eyes and eyelids now. Your eyelids are so heavy and smooth. Flowing up into your eyebrows, over your forehead, over the top of your head, down the back of your head, and down the back of your neck.

A new heaviness is starting in your toes now. Twice as heavy as the first time. Imagine a heavy weight on each toe. Feel the heaviness deep and even more relaxed. And this heavy, deep feeling is going into your feet, your ankles, your calves, your knees, going into your thighs, your hips, into your waist. Flowing up into your chest now, relaxing your heart, relaxing your lungs, allowing your breathing to be more intense, more regular, more and more completely relaxed. Now the deep heavy feeling is flowing into your shoulders, and down your arms, your upper arms, your forearms, into your hands and fingers. And now flowing back through your forearms, your upper arms, into your shoulders and into your neck. Flowing over your face, into your eyes, over your eyebrows, over your forehead, over the top of your head, down the back of your head and down the back of your neck.

And a new heaviness is starting now at the top of your head. Twice as heavy as before. Twice as heavy. Imagine a heavy weight on the very top of your head, soft and relaxed and heavy. Feel the heavy relaxation flowing down into your face and eyes now, down through your neck, your shoulders, flowing down through your chest, your waist, your hips, your thighs, your knees, into your calves, your ankles, your feet and toes. Deeply relaxed, loose and limp, and comfortable from the top of your head to the very tip of your toes.

I want you to imagine now that you are looking at a blackboard. On the blackboard imagine a circle. Into the circle we are going to place the letters of the alphabet in reverse order, and with each letter after you place it into the circle, you will erase it then from inside the circle and allow yourself to relax more and more deeply.

Picture the blackboard now. Picture the circle. Into the circle put the letter Z. Now erase the Z from inside the circle, and go deeper. Put Y into the circle, and erase it and go deeper. X, and erase it and go deeper still. W, and erase it. V, and erase it. U, and erase it. T, and erase it. S, and erase it. R, and erase it. Q, and erase it. P, and erase it. O, and erase it. N, and erase it. M, and erase it. L, and erase it. K, and erase it. J, and erase it. I, and erase it. H, and erase it. G, and erase it. F, and erase it. E, and erase it. D, and erase it. C, and erase it. B, and erase it. A, and erase it. Now erase the circle and forget about the blackboard. Just go on relaxing more and more deeply. Feel yourself sink into the chair, mind and body drifting deeper and deeper into relaxation, deeper with each breath.

As you breathe in, imagine that you are breathing in a pure clean, odorless anesthesia. The anesthesia is flowing all throughout your body now. It is a warm, numb, tingling feeling, and the more you breathe in, the more you want to breathe in, and you allow your breathing to become even deeper now, bringing in more and more of this peaceful, relaxing, tranquil feeling. From now on until the end of this session, you will allow yourself to relax more and more completely with each breath you take.

I want you to imagine now that you are looking at a clear, blue summer sky. And in the sky, a sky-writing airplane is writing your first name in fluffy, white cloud-like letters. See your name floating fluffy, white, and cloud-like in a clear, blue sky. Now let your name just dissolve away. Let the winds just blow your name away into the blue. Forget about your name. Forget you even have a name. Names are not important. Just go on listening to my voice and allowing yourself to relax more deeply.

I want you to imagine now that you are standing on the top step of a heavy wooden staircase. Feel the carpet under your feet. Now extend your hand out and touch the railing. Feel the smooth polished wood of the railing under your hand. You are standing just ten steps up from the floor below. The stairs are curving very smoothly down to the floor below. In a moment we will walk down the stairs. With each step down you will allow yourself to relax even more deeply. By the time you reach the floor below you will be deeper than you have ever gone before. Take a step down now, down to the ninth step smoothly and easily. Feel yourself going deeper. Now down to 8, deeper still. Now down to 7...6...5...4...3...2...1. Now you are standing on the floor below. There is a door in front of you. The sign on the door reads, "Doorway to the Beach of Time." Reach out and open the door. A stream of golden sunlight pours through the open door. Walk through the door into the golden sunlight.

Before you stretches a beach of gleaming white sand. Beyond the edge of the beach is an endless ocean of clear blue-green water. Walk forward on the beach until you come to the place where the dry sand meets the wet sand near the water's edge. Stand here a moment and absorb all the sights and sounds.

This is the beach of time, and the ocean before you is the infinite sea of never-ending life and consciousness. You have been here before.

The sea gulls circle in the sky above and dive for their dinner in the sea below, chattering as they return to the sky. Notice the other birds around you.

The warm sun feels good. Notice that you are completely enveloped in your powerful positive energy field of white light that protects you from the effects of all negative external influences.

Turn your head to the right and observe the door of the past just a short way up the beach. The door is open just as you left it on your last visit here. Beyond the door observe the silver fog bank that is currently blocking your view.

In a few moments we will go through that door and regress into past times in your current life.

If an emergency should occur in the present time that requires your immediate presence and awareness, your mind will immediately pull you from the regression back into the present time and into conscious awareness so that you can deal with the emergency situation. You will not experience any harmful or uncomfortable side effects from being pulled immediately back into current time and awareness.

Now turn and walk up to the door of the past, but do not enter just yet.

In a few moments when you walk through the door, I will guide you through time by a series of instructions. I will signal my instructions by counting one, two, three and then snapping my fingers. Like this: one, two, three. (Snap) The counting followed by the finger snapping signals your mind to take you to a different time or place as I instruct.

Later I will tell you to direct yourself to select a time or place and regress yourself to it. You will do it the same way I have done it. You may either count one, two, three and snap your fingers, or you may count one, two, three and say GO if you do not wish to snap your fingers. Either method works just fine. Let us practice it now before we enter through the door to the past.

Mentally say to yourself one, two, three and snap your fingers.

(Pause 5 seconds.)

Now mentally say to yourself one, two, three and mentally say GO.

(Pause 5 seconds.)

Now it is an established fact. Whenever you wish to change the time or place during regression all you need to do is either mentally count to three and snap your fingers or else mentally count to three and mentally say GO. You will learn how to use this signal very shortly.

During your trips into your past I will ask you questions. When I ask you questions, I want you to answer out loud if you want even though you are alone. Answering out loud enables you to better recall the information when you return to the present time. If you do not wish to answer out loud then answer mentally. But be sure to answer the questions and not ignore them. That way you will have a more successful regression and you will have better recall when you return to present time.

Now mentally say to yourself, "I am ready to enter the past, and I want to enter the past."

Now step through the door and walk into the fog bank.

(Pause 3 seconds.)

You may stop walking now. You are completely surrounded by refreshing, cool, damp fog.

At the moment you can see nothing except the silver fog.

In a moment I am going to count to three and snap my fingers. When I do, you will start moving backward in time. You will feel the fog moving rapidly past you indicating your movement back in time.

One, two, three.

(Snap.)

Feel the fog moving rapidly past you now as you go back in time. You can sense shadowy images of people and events in the fog flying past you as you regress further backward.

I am going to count to three and snap my fingers. When I do, the movement will stop. One, two, three.

(Snap.)

You have now stopped at a past time in your current life. The fog still surrounds you. I will count to three and snap my fingers and the fog will disappear and you will find yourself eating your main meal yesterday. One, two, three.

(Snap.)

The fog is gone and you are eating your main meal yesterday.

What day is it?

What is the date?

What time is it?

Look around you. Observe all the details. the smells. the colors. the surroundings.

What are you wearing?
Is anyone with you?
Who?
If there are other people, what are they wearing?
Where are you?
How do you feel? Are you happy? Are you sad?
Is there any conversation? If so, what is being said and by whom? Take your time and observe everything and tell everything that is happening.

(Pause 10 seconds.)

Is there more you can tell me about where you are and what is happening? Take your time. Observe and report everything you see.

(Pause 10 seconds.)

Observe and report everything you feel.

(Pause 10 seconds.)

Observe and report everything you are experiencing.

(Pause 10 seconds.)

Observe and report everything you hear.

(Pause 10 seconds.)

In a moment I am going to count to three and snap my fingers. When I do your present experience will disappear and it will be noontime on your last birthday. One, two, three.

(Snap.)

It is now noontime on your last birthday.
What day is it?
Where are you?

Are you alone or with other people?

Take your time and observe and experience all details and report them.

(Pause 10 seconds.)

What do you see?

(Pause 10 seconds.)

What do you feel?

(Pause 10 seconds.)

What do you hear?

(Pause 10 seconds.)

What action is taking place?

(Pause 10 seconds.)

Take your time and describe the entire experience you are now having.

(Pause 15 seconds.)

In a few moments I will count to three and snap my fingers. At that time it will be five hours later. One, two, three.

(Snap.)

It is now five hours later.

Where are you?

What time is it?

Take your time and completely describe everything in detail without any prompting from me. I will stop talking for one minute while you experience what is happening now.

(Pause 60 seconds.)

I am now going to count to three and snap my fingers. When I do, it will be ten years earlier. One, two, three.

(Snap.)

Where are you now?
What are you doing?
What are you wearing?
How do you feel?
What do you see?
Is anyone with you?
What do you hear?

I am going to give you one minute now to describe your experience. Give details.

(Pause 60 seconds.)

I am going to count to three and snap my fingers. When I do you will be back in the fog bank of time. One, two, three.

(Snap.)

You are now back in the fog bank of time, completely surrounded by cool, moist silver fog.

In a few moments I am going to ask you to direct yourself to another period in this same lifetime. You can do it the same way I have just done it for you. Select any time you wish and then mentally count to three and either snap your fingers or say GO just as you practiced before. When you get there, if the fog is still present you can get rid of it by counting to three and either snapping your fingers or mentally saying GO just as you have done before. I will give you two minutes to do this before you again hear my voice.

Do it now. Take yourself to another period in this lifetime. And please report everything that happens. Now GO.

(Pause 120 seconds.)

Very good. Now when I count to three and snap my fingers you will be back to your birth just one minute after you have left your mother's body. One, two, three.

(Snap.)

Absorb all the sights, sounds, and smells. What time is it?
What day is it?
Who is present besides yourself?
Describe the experience completely. Take your time. I will give you one minute.

(Pause 60 seconds.)

I am now going to count to three and snap my fingers. When I do it will be one year later. One, two, three.

(Snap.)

Describe your experience now. Give all the details. You have one minute.

(Pause 60 seconds.)

Now take yourself to a day in this lifetime when you were the happiest that you have ever been. Do it now.

(Pause 5 seconds.)

Where are you? What is happening? Describe the entire experience in detail. You have one minute.

(Pause 60 seconds.)

It will now be one hour later. One, two, three.

(Snap.)

It is now one hour later. What are you experiencing? Now go to five days earlier. One, two, three.

(Snap.)

It is now five days earlier. What are you experiencing?

Now return to the fog bank of time. One, two, three.

(Snap.)

You are now back in the fog bank of time.
Time will now move forward. One, two, three.

(Snap.)

Time is now moving forward. Feel the rapid movement of fog past you. Notice the shadowy figures of people and events moving rapidly past you.

Time will now stop. One, two, three.

(Snap.)

The movement of time has stopped.
Now return to the beach of time. One, two, three.

(Snap.)

You are now standing back on the beach of time in the present moment as the fog bank disappears.

Now you will return to the bottom of your staircase. One, two, three.

(Snap.)

You are now at the foot of your spiral staircase. I will now count from one to ten. With each number

I say, take one step up your staircase until you reach the top.

1...2...3...4...5...6...7...8...9...10.

You are now at the top of your staircase. Whenever you wish to enter the beach of time all you need to do is to come to your staircase, walk down the stairs, and go through the door to the beach just as you have experienced moments ago.

You have just learned how to go to the beach of time, go through the door to the past and regress to any time you wish within your current lifetime and then return to the current moment. You learned how to signal yourself to change events, time, and places by counting to three and either snapping your fingers or saying GO. You had the experience of me directing you through regressions, and you had the experience of directing yourself through regressions.

During this regression session, you noticed that I shortened my signaling to you and showed you how rapidly it is possible to change time. You are now ready to go back in time to previous lifetimes and experience who you have been before this lifetime.

If you are in an altered state of consciousness or in a past life experience and an emergency situation should occur in your current lifetime that requires your immediate presence and awareness, your mind will immediately pull you from the regression and altered state back into your current life and conscious awareness so you can deal with the emergency situation. This important safeguard is now programmed into your mind permanently for your benefit and welfare. You will not experience any harmful or uncomfortable side effects from being pulled immediately back to current time and awareness.

The next time you hear my voice, you will allow yourself to relax ten times more deeply than you are now and the suggestions I give you then will go ten times deeper into every level of your mind.

In a few moments you will awaken yourself. When you awaken you will feel great. Full of energy and enthusiasm. You will feel simply terrific, and you will continue to feel terrific all the rest of the day. You will remember everything that happened during your regressions. All you need to do to awaken yourself is to count mentally with me as I count from one to five and then open your eyes.

1...2...coming up slowly now. 3...4...5.

(Snap.)

Open eyes, wide awake, feeling fine.

(Turn off tape recorder.)

Take the time to write or record your experiences during your regression with Tape Two.

The tape guided you through the procedure for altering your state of consciousness and entering and leaving past experiences. You have been programmed with an important safeguard in the event an emergency situation occurs while you are in an altered state of consciousness. You have been given a powerful positive energy shield to protect you from the effects of external negative influences. You have learned how to trigger changes by counting to three and snapping your fingers or saying GO. You have been given the post-hypnotic suggestion to go ten times deeper the next time you hear your voice.

Now you are ready to regress to previous lifetimes. Tape Three will guide you to several experiences in previous lifetimes.

You may play Tape Three any time you wish now. My recommendation is that you wait for at least an hour while you get up and move around and do something else—your body will appreciate the break. I also recommend that you do not wait more than a week before playing Tape Three. This is so you can get maximum benefit from the suggestions given you in Tape Two. Hypnotic suggestions tend to weaken over a period of time.

PAST LIFE REGRESSION

In a few moments Tape Three will guide you into a deeply relaxing and peaceful altered state of consciousness. Then you will be guided into a series of regressions into several of your past lives—lives you lived before your current life. The tape will also give you the opportunity to direct yourself to several past life experiences.

In at least one of the regressions, you will be directed to a past lifetime where you knew someone who you also know in this current lifetime. I suggest that you have the name in mind of someone you currently feel very close to such as a spouse, child, close friend, brother, or sister. Keep that name in your mind because the voice on the tape will say, "You will now go back to a lifetime where you knew the person you have in mind, and you will be with that person."

If you do many regressions, you will likely meet a number of people who you know in this current life. You will recognize them even though they look different, have different names, possibly even be a different sex, and may have an entirely different relationship to you than they have now.

When you use this tape, you will be asking yourself a number of questions, such as "Who are you?" "Observe and report everything you are experiencing." "Is anyone with you?" and so forth. Answer these questions out loud. Keep a pen or pencil and writing paper handy so you can record your regression experiences after you return to the present time. If you prefer, have a blank tape on hand to put into your tape recorder so you can verbally record your experiences afterward.

Now find a comfortable position for you to sit or lie in for about thirty-five minutes.

Tape Three (recording script)

Close your eyes. Take a deep, full breath and exhale slowly. Take another deep breath and exhale. One more time a deep, full breath and hold it in. Now let it out completely and feel yourself relaxing more.

I want you to imagine now that all your tensions, all your tightness, and all your fears and worries are draining away from the top of your head. Let it drain down through your face, down through your neck, through your shoulders, through your chest, your waist, your hips, your thighs, down through your knees, your calves, your ankles, your feet and out your toes. All your tension, all your tightness, all your worries and fears are draining away now from the very tips of your toes, and you are relaxing more and more.

Focus your attention on your toes now and allow your toes to relax completely. Each toe is loose and heavy. Now let this relaxation flow into your feet, into your ankles, your calves, your knees. Feel it flowing into your thighs, into your hips, into your waist, flowing up into your chest now. Feel your breathing easier and deeper, more regular and more relaxed. Now let the deep relaxed feeling go into your shoulders, down your arms, into your upper arms, your forearms, and into your hands and fingers, and flowing back into your forearms, your upper arms, your shoulders. Flowing into your neck, over your face, your chin, your cheeks, even your ears are relaxed. Feel it flowing into your eyes and eyelids now. Your eyelids are so heavy and smooth. Flowing up into your eyebrows, over your forehead, over the top of your head, down the back of your head, and down the back of your neck.

A new heaviness is starting in your toes now. Twice as heavy as the first time. Imagine a heavy weight on each toe. Feel the heaviness deep and even more relaxed. And this heavy, deep feeling is going into your feet, your ankles, your calves, your knees, going into your thighs, your hips, into your waist. Flowing up into your chest now, relaxing your heart, relaxing your lungs, allowing your breathing to be more intense, more regular, more and more completely relaxed. Now the deep heavy feeling is flowing into your shoulders, and down your arms, your upper arms, your forearms, into your hands and fingers. And now flowing back through your forearms, your upper arms, into your shoulders and into your neck. Flowing over your face, into your eyes, over your eyebrows, over your forehead, over the top of your head, down the back of your head and down the back of your neck.

And a new heaviness is starting now at the top of your head. Twice as heavy as before. Twice as heavy. Imagine a heavy weight on the very top of your head, soft and relaxed and heavy. Feel the heavy relaxation flowing down into your face and eyes now, down through your neck, your shoulders, flowing down through your chest, your waist, your hips, your thighs, your knees, into your calves, your ankles, your feet and toes. Deeply relaxed, loose and limp, and comfortable from the top of your head to the very tip of your toes.

I want you to imagine now that you are looking at a blackboard. On the blackboard imagine a circle. Into the circle we are going to place the letters of the alphabet in reverse order, and with each letter after you place it into the circle, you will erase it then from inside the circle and allow yourself to relax more and more deeply.

Picture the blackboard now. Picture the circle. Into the circle put the letter Z. Now erase the Z from inside the circle, and go deeper. Put Y into the circle, and erase it and go deeper. X, and erase it and go deeper still. W, and erase it. V, and erase it. U, and erase it. T, and erase it. S, and erase it. R, and erase it. Q, and erase it. P, and erase it. O, and erase it. N, and erase it. M, and erase it. L, and erase it. K, and erase it. J, and erase it. I, and erase it. H, and erase it. G, and erase it. F, and erase it. E, and erase it. D, and erase it. C, and erase it. B, and erase it. A, and erase it. Now erase the circle and forget about the blackboard. Just go on relaxing more and more deeply. Feel yourself sink into the chair, mind and body drifting deeper and deeper into relaxation, deeper with each breath.

As you breathe in, imagine that you are breathing in a pure clean, odorless anesthesia. The anesthesia is flowing all throughout your body now. It is a warm, numb, tingling feeling, and the more you breathe in, the more you want to breathe in, and you allow your breathing to become even deeper now, bringing in more and more of this peaceful, relaxing, tranquil feeling. From now on until the end of this session, you will allow yourself to relax more and more completely with each breath you take.

I want you to imagine now that you are looking at a clear, blue summer sky. And in the sky, a sky-writing airplane is writing your first name in fluffy, white cloud-like letters. See your name floating fluffy, white, and cloud-like in a clear, blue sky. Now let your name just dissolve away. Let the winds just blow your name away into the blue. Forget about your name. Forget you even have a name. Names are not important. Just go on listening to my voice and allowing yourself to relax more deeply.

I want you to imagine now that you are standing on the top step of a heavy wooden staircase. Feel the carpet under your feet. Now extend your hand out and touch the railing. Feel the smooth polished wood of the railing under your hand. You are standing just ten steps up from the floor below. The stairs are curving very smoothly down to the floor below. In a moment we will walk down the stairs. With each step down you will allow yourself to relax even more deeply. By the time you reach the floor below you will be deeper than you have ever gone before. Take a step down now, down to the ninth step smoothly and easily. Feel yourself going deeper. Now down to 8, deeper still. Now down to 7...6...5...4...3...2...1. Now you are standing on the floor below. There is a door in front of you. The sign on the door reads, "Doorway to the Beach of Time." Reach out and open the door. A stream of golden sunlight pours through the open door. Walk through the door into the golden sunlight.

Before you stretches a beach of gleaming white sand. Beyond the edge of the beach is an endless ocean of clear blue-green water. Walk forward on the beach until you come to the place where the dry sand meets the wet sand near the water's edge. Stand here a moment and absorb all the sights and sounds.

This is the beach of time, and the ocean before you is the infinite sea of never-ending life and consciousness. You have been here before.

The sea gulls circle in the sky above and dive for their dinner in the sea below, chattering as they return to the sky. Notice the other birds around you.

The warm sun feels good. Notice that you are completely enveloped in your powerful positive energy field of white light that protects you from the effects of all negative external influences.

Turn your head to the right and observe the door of the past just a short way up the beach. The door is open just as you left it on your last visit here. Beyond the door observe the silver fog bank that is currently blocking your view.

In a few moments we will go through that door and regress into past lives; lives you lived before this current life.

If an emergency should occur in the present time that requires your immediate presence and awareness, your mind will immediately pull you from the regression back into the present time and into conscious awareness so that you can deal with the emergency situation. You will not experience any harmful or uncomfortable side effects from being pulled immediately back into current time and awareness.

Now turn and walk up to the door of the past, but do not enter just yet.

In a few moments when you walk through the door, I will guide you through time by a series of instructions. I will signal my instructions by counting to three and snapping my fingers just as I have done before on your previous regression experiences. The counting followed by the finger snapping signals your mind to take you to a different time or place as I instruct.

Later I will tell you to direct yourself to select a time or place and regress yourself to it. You will do it the same way I have done it. You may either count to three and snap your fingers or you may count to three and say GO if you do not wish to snap your fingers. Either method works just fine. Do it just as you did when you regressed yourself previously.

During your trips into your past lives I will ask you questions. When I ask you questions, I want you to *answer out loud if you want even though you are alone. Answering out loud enables you to better recall the information when you return to the present time. If you do not wish to answer out loud then answer mentally. But be sure to answer the questions and not ignore them. That way you will have a more successful regression and you will have better recall when you return to present time.*

You will recall all your regression experiences when you return to the present time.

Now mentally say to yourself, "I am ready to enter the past, and I want to enter the past."

Now step through the door and walk into the fog bank.

(Pause 3 seconds.)

You may stop walking now. You are completely surrounded by refreshing, cool, damp fog.

At the moment you can see nothing except the silver fog.

In a moment I am going to count to three and snap my fingers. When I do, you will start moving backward in time. You will feel the fog moving rapidly past you indicating your movement back in time.

One, two, three.

(Snap.)

Feel the fog moving rapidly past you now as you go back in time. You can sense shadowy images of people and events in the fog moving past you as you regress further backward. You are moving faster now. Further and further back in time toward one of your previous lives.

When I count to three and snap my fingers, the movement will stop and you will find yourself in a past lifetime where you were very happy. One, two, three.

(Snap.)

The fog still surrounds you. The fog will now disappear. One, two, three.

(Snap.)

The fog is gone, and you can see and experience this lifetime.

Who are you?

What is your name?

Are you male or female?

Where are you?

What are you doing?

What day is it?

What is the date?

What time is it?

Look around you. Observe all the details. the smells. the colors. the surroundings.

What are you wearing?

Is anyone with you?

Who?

If there are other people, what are they wearing?

How do you feel? Are you happy? What makes you so happy?

Is there any conversation? If so, what is being said?

Take your time and observe everything.

(Pause 10 seconds.)

Is there more you can tell me about where you are and who you are and what is happening? Take your time. Observe and report everything you see.

(Pause 10 seconds.)

Observe and report everything you feel.

(Pause 10 seconds.)

Observe and report everything you are experiencing.

(Pause 10 seconds.)

Observe and report everything you hear.

(Pause 10 seconds.)

In a moment I am going to count to three and snap my fingers. When I do it will be one year later. One, two, three.

(Snap.)

It is now one year later.
What day is it?
Where are you?
Are you alone or with other people?
Take your time and observe and experience all details and report them.

(Pause 10 seconds.)

What do you see?

(Pause 10 seconds.)

What do you feel?

(Pause 10 seconds.)

What do you hear?

(Pause 10 seconds.)

What action is taking place?

(Pause 10 seconds.)

Take your time and describe the entire experience you are now having.

(Pause 15 seconds.)

In a few moments I will count to three and snap my fingers. At that time it will be five years later. One, two, three.

(Snap.)

It is now five years later.
Where are you?
What time is it?
Take your time and completely describe everything in detail without any prompting from me. I will stop talking for one minute while you experience what is happening.

(Pause 60 seconds.)

I am now going to count to three and snap my fingers. When I do, it will be ten years earlier. One, two, three.

(Snap.)

Where are you now?
What are you doing?
What are you wearing?
How do you feel?
What do you see?
Is anyone with you?
What do you hear?

I am going to give you one minute now to describe your experience. Give details.

(Pause 60 seconds.)

I am going to count to three and snap my fingers. When I do you will be back in the fog bank of time. One, two, three.

(Snap.)

You are now back in the fog bank of time completely surrounded by cool, moist silver fog.

In a few moments I am going to ask you to direct yourself to another lifetime where you knew the person you have in mind, and you will be with that person. You can do it the same way I have just done it for you. Just mentally say that you wish to go to a lifetime where you knew the person you have in mind and to be with that person. Then count to three and either snap your fingers or say GO just as you practiced before. When you get there, if the fog is still present, you can get rid of it by counting to three and either snapping your fingers or mentally saying GO just as you have done before. The fog will then disappear and you will be with the person you have in mind. I will give you two minutes to do this before you again hear my voice. Do it now. And please report everything that happens. Now GO.

(Pause 120 seconds.)

Very good. Who are you? Who is with you? Where are you?

(Pause 15 seconds.)

You will now return to the fog bank of time. One, two, three.

(Snap.)

You are now back in the fog bank of time.

Now when I count to three and snap my fingers you will go to a past lifetime that relates in some important way to your current lifetime. One, two, three.

(Snap.)

Where are you?
Who are you?
Absorb all the sights, sounds, and smells. What time is it?
What day is it?
What year is it?
Is anyone with you?
Describe the experience completely. Take your time. Why is this an important lifetime for you? Search for answers. I will give you one minute.

(Pause 60 seconds.)

When I count to three and snap my fingers it will be one year later. One, two, three.

(Snap.)

Describe your experience now. Give all the details. You have one minute.

(Pause 60 seconds.)

Now you direct yourself to a day in this lifetime when you were the happiest that you have ever been. Do it now.

(Pause 5 seconds.)

Where are you? What is happening? Describe the entire experience in detail. You have one minute.

(Pause 60 seconds.)

When I count to three and snap my fingers it will be five minutes before your death from this lifetime. One, two, three.

(Snap.)

It is now five minutes before your death in this lifetime. What are you experiencing?

(Pause 15 seconds.)

I will now direct you to the other side of this death experience. It will be one hour later. One, two, three.

(Snap.)

It is now one hour later. What are you experiencing?

(Pause 15 seconds.)

When I count to three and snap my fingers you will be back in the fog bank of time. One, two, three.

(Snap.)

You are now back in the fog bank of time.
Time will now move forward. One, two, three.

(Snap.)

Time is now moving forward. Feel the rapid movement of fog past you. Notice the shadowy figures of people and events moving rapidly past you.
Now time will stop. One, two, three.

(Snap.)

The movement of time has stopped.
Now return to the beach of time. One, two, three.

(Snap.)

You are now standing back on the beach of time in the present moment as the fog bank disappears.

You will now go to the foot of your staircase. One, two, three.

(Snap.)

You are now at the foot of your spiral staircase. I will now count from one to ten. With each number I say, take one step up your staircase until you reach the top.

1...2...3...4...5...6...7...8...9...10.

You are now at the top of your staircase. Whenever you wish to enter the beach of time, all you need to do is to come to your staircase, walk down the stairs, and go through the door to the beach just as you have experienced moments ago.

You have just learned how to go to the beach of time, go through the door to the past, and regress to any previous lifetime time you wish and then return to the current moment. You had the experience of me directing you through regressions, and you had the experience of directing yourself through regressions.

You are now ready to direct yourself back in time to previous lifetimes and experience who you have been before this lifetime.

If an emergency situation should occur in your current lifetime when you are in an altered state of consciousness or in a past life experience, your mind will immediately pull you back into your current life and conscious awareness so you can deal with the emergency situation. This important safeguard is now programmed into your mind permanently for your benefit and welfare. You will not experience any harmful or uncomfortable side effects from being pulled immediately back to current time and awareness.

The next time you hear my voice you will allow yourself to relax ten times more deeply than you are now and the suggestions I give you then will go ten times deeper into every level of your mind.

In a few moments you will awaken yourself. When you awaken you will feel great. Full of energy and enthusiasm. You will feel simply terrific, and you will continue to feel terrific all the rest of the day. You will remember everything that happened during your regressions. All you need to do to awaken yourself is to count mentally with me as I count from one to five and then open your eyes.

1...2...coming up slowly now. 3...4...5.

(Snap.)

Open eyes, wide awake, feeling fine.

(Turn off tape recorder.)

Take time now to write down or record your experiences during Tape Three.

The tape guided you through the procedure for altering your state of consciousness and entering and leaving past experiences. It also programmed you with an important safeguard in the event an emergency situation occurs while you are in an altered state of consciousness. You have been given a powerful positive energy shield to protect you from the effects of external negative influences. You have learned how to trigger changes by counting to three and snapping your fingers or saying GO. You have been given the post-hypnotic suggestion to go ten times deeper the next time you hear your voice.

Now you are ready to experience your own self-directed regression to previous lifetimes. Tape Four guides you to the fog bank of time. From that point on you will no longer hear directions from the tape. You will be on your own. You have no need for concern because you are trained now, and you have experience.

If you feel you want more training and experience before going on to Tape Four, go through any or all of the other tapes.

In Tape Three you experienced brief glimpses of several past lifetimes. When you begin your self-directed regression, you will be able to stay as long as you wish in any particular lifetime so you can gain a more thorough experience than you had during this training session. You may want to plan out your self-regression trips in advance in order to have a more meaningful experience.

You may play Tape Four anytime you wish now. My recommendation is that you wait for at least an hour while you get up and move around and do something else—your body will appreciate the break. I also recommend that you do not wait more than a week before playing Tape Four. This is so you can get maximum benefit from the suggestions given you in Tape Three. Hypnotic suggestions tend to weaken over a period of time.

Self-Directed Regression

Tape Four guides you into a deeply relaxing and peaceful altered state of consciousness. Then it guides you through the doorway of the past into the fog bank of time. At that point the voice on the tape will stop talking, and you will take over completely and direct yourself through past life regressions for as long as you wish. You can regress in this current life or in previous lives. You can select one life or period or several. The choice is yours. You have received all the training you need from the first three tapes. Now all you need to do is get firsthand experience by guiding yourself through past time travel just as the words guided you in the first three tapes.

For all future regressions, all you need is Tape Four. However, if you wish to refresh or reinforce yourself with any of the first three tapes, do so.

Remember, the more you engage in regression experiences, the more proficient you will become and the more vivid the experiences.

When you reach the point where the voice on the tape stops talking and you take total control, do not be concerned about your tape player. Just let it continue to run because the rest of the tape is blank. It will automatically shut off by itself at the end of the tape.

Keep a pen or pencil and writing paper handy so you can record your regression experiences after you return to the present time. If you prefer, have a blank tape ready to put into your tape recorder so you can verbally record your experiences afterward.

Now find a comfortable position for you to sit or lie in for a long period of time because you will be directing your own past life regression for as long a period of time as you wish.

Tape Four (recording script)

Close your eyes. Take a deep, full breath and exhale slowly. Take another deep breath and exhale. One more time a deep, full breath and hold it in. Now let it out completely and feel yourself relaxing more.

I want you to imagine now that all your tensions, all your tightness, and all your fears and worries are draining away from the top of your head. Let it drain down through your face, down through your neck, through your shoulders, through your chest, your waist, your hips, your thighs, down through your knees, your calves, your ankles, your feet and out your toes. All your tension, all your tightness, all your worries and fears are draining away now from the very tips of your toes, and you are relaxing more and more.

Focus your attention on your toes now and allow your toes to relax completely. Each toe is loose and heavy. Now let this relaxation flow into your feet, into your ankles, your calves, your knees. Feel it flowing into your thighs, into your hips, into your waist, flowing up into your chest now. Feel your breathing easier and deeper, more regular and more relaxed. Now let the deep relaxed feeling go into your shoulders, down your arms, into your upper arms, your forearms, and into your hands and fingers, and flowing back into your forearms, your upper arms, your shoulders. Flowing into your neck, over your face, your chin, your cheeks, even your ears are relaxed. Feel it flowing into your eyes and eyelids now. Your eyelids are so heavy and smooth. Flowing up into your eyebrows, over your forehead, over the top of your head, down the back of your head, and down the back of your neck.

A new heaviness is starting in your toes now. Twice as heavy as the first time. Imagine a heavy weight on each toe. Feel the heaviness deep and even more relaxed. And this heavy, deep feeling is going into your feet, your ankles, your calves, your knees, going into your thighs, your hips, into your waist. Flowing up into your chest now, relaxing your heart, relaxing your lungs, allowing your breathing to be more intense, more regular, more and more completely relaxed. Now the deep heavy feeling is flowing into your shoulders, and down your arms, your upper arms, your forearms, into your hands and fingers. And now flowing back through your forearms, your upper arms, into your shoulders and into your neck. Flowing over your face, into your eyes, over your eyebrows, over your forehead, over the top of your head, down the back of your head and down the back of your neck.

And a new heaviness is starting now at the top of your head. Twice as heavy as before. Twice as heavy. Imagine a heavy weight on the very top of your head, soft and relaxed and heavy. Feel the heavy relaxation flowing down into your face and eyes now, down through your neck, your shoulders, flowing down through your chest, your waist, your hips, your thighs, your knees, into your calves, your ankles, your feet and toes. Deeply relaxed, loose and limp, and comfortable from the top of your head to the very tip of your toes.

I want you to imagine now that you are looking at a blackboard. On the blackboard imagine a circle. Into the circle we are going to place the letters of the alphabet in reverse order, and with each letter after you place it into the circle, you will erase it then from inside the circle and allow yourself to relax more and more deeply.

Picture the blackboard now. Picture the circle. Into the circle put the letter Z. Now erase the Z from inside the circle, and go deeper. Put Y into the circle, and erase it and go deeper. X, and erase it and go deeper still. W, and erase it. V, and erase it. U, and erase it. T, and erase it. S, and erase it. R, and erase it. Q, and erase it. P, and erase it. O, and erase it. N, and erase it. M, and erase it. L, and erase it. K, and erase it. J, and erase it. I, and erase it. H, and erase it. G, and erase it. F, and erase it. E, and erase it. D, and erase it. C, and erase it. B, and erase it. A, and erase it. Now erase the circle and forget about the blackboard. Just go on relaxing more and more deeply. Feel yourself sink into the chair, mind and body drifting deeper and deeper into relaxation, deeper with each breath.

As you breathe in, imagine that you are breathing in a pure clean, odorless anesthesia. The anesthesia is flowing all throughout your body now. It is a warm, numb, tingling feeling, and the more you breathe in, the more you want to breathe in, and you allow your breathing to become even deeper now, bringing in more and more of this peaceful, relaxing, tranquil feeling. From now on until the end of this session, you will allow yourself to relax more and more completely with each breath you take.

I want you to imagine now that you are looking at a clear, blue summer sky. And in the sky, a sky-writing airplane is writing your first name in fluffy, white cloud-like letters. See your name floating fluffy, white, and cloud-like in a clear, blue sky. Now let your name just dissolve away. Let the winds just blow your name away into the blue. Forget about your name. Forget you even have a name. Names are not important. Just go on listening to my voice and allowing yourself to relax more deeply.

I want you to imagine now that you are standing on the top step of a heavy wooden staircase. Feel the carpet under your feet. Now extend your hand out and touch the railing. Feel the smooth polished wood of the railing under your hand. You are standing just ten steps up from the floor below. The stairs are curving very smoothly down to the floor below. In a moment we will walk down the stairs. With each step down you will allow yourself to relax even more deeply. By the time you reach the floor below you will be deeper than you have ever gone before. Take a step down now, down to the ninth step smoothly and easily. Feel yourself going deeper. Now down to 8, deeper still. Now down to 7...6...5...4...3...2...1. Now you are standing on the floor below. There is a door in front of you. The sign on the door reads, "Doorway to the Beach of Time." Reach out and open the door. A stream of golden sunlight pours through the open door. Walk through the door into the golden sunlight.

Before you stretches a beach of gleaming white sand. Beyond the edge of the beach is an endless ocean of clear blue- green water. Walk forward on the beach until you come to the place where the dry sand meets the wet sand near the water's edge. Stand here a moment and absorb all the sights and sounds.

This is the beach of time, and the ocean before you is the infinite sea of never-ending life and consciousness. You have been here before.

The sea gulls circle in the sky above and dive for their dinner in the sea below, chattering as they return to the sky. Notice the other birds around you.

The warm sun feels good. Notice that you are completely enveloped in your powerful positive energy field of white light that protects you from the effects of all negative external influences.

Turn your head to the right and observe the door of the past just a short way up the beach. The door is open just as you left it on your last visit here. Beyond the door observe the silver fog bank that is currently blocking your view.

In a few moments we will go through that door and you will regress yourself into past times.

If an emergency should occur in the present time that requires your immediate presence and awareness, your mind will immediately pull you from the regression back into the present time and into conscious awareness so that you can deal with the emergency situation. You will not experience any harmful or uncomfortable side effects from being pulled immediately back into current time and awareness.

Now turn and walk up to the door of the past, but do not enter just yet.

Shortly after you walk through the door, I will stop talking and will turn total control over to you. You can

*control your movement through time by either count-
ing to three and snapping your fingers, or by counting
to three and saying GO just as you learned and practiced before.*

*Be observant of everything you experience. Look for
details. Make mental note of your feelings, what you
see, what you hear, and what is going on. Make mental note of the date and time. Of colors and environment. Absorb the complete experience so you can
record it after you bring yourself back to the current
time.*

*You will have total recall of all your experiences
when you return to current time.*

*The next time you hear my voice, you will allow
yourself to relax ten times more deeply than you are
now, and the suggestions I give you then will go ten
times deeper into every level of your mind.*

*Now mentally say to yourself, "I am ready to enter
the past, and I want to enter the past."*

*Now step through the door and walk into the fog
bank.*

(Pause 3 seconds.)

*You may stop walking now. You are completely sur-
rounded by refreshing, cool, damp fog.*

*At the moment you can see nothing except the sil-
ver fog.*

*Now I am going to stop talking. You can now take
total control. Begin your journey back in time. Have a
nice trip.*

(Turn off tape recorder; keep the rest of the tape blank.)

Some people who use this self-hypnosis regression procedures may have such extensive, detailed experiences that they may have good material to write a magazine article or book.

Some may find answers to questions they have about their current lifetime.

Most at least should have an enjoyable time, and learn something in the process.

As a bonus, you can go to the beach of time and just stay there in the present moment while meditating, praying, programming goals, relaxing, or whatever you wish.

Part III

Practical Applications and Supplemental Information

Chapter 9

Suggestions

This chapter contains a collection of suggestions appropriate for a variety of purposes. Use the explanations and wording of each suggestion on your clients or on yourself in self-hypnosis. Although this list isn't all inclusive, it provides you with a start upon which you can enlarge or modify for your specific needs.

Strengthening Your Aura

Your aura radiates from you with the strength and colors that you decide by your mental, physical, and emotional condition. You choose to be in such a positive, healthy, balanced state that your aura is powerful, clear, and brilliant with the beneficial energy you desire.

Visualize your aura as you wish it to be and command your higher self with these words: "I am now becoming the kind of person I need to be to radiate the aura I visualize and desire."

Improving Concentration and Memory

You will feel a tremendous and intense concentration power with everything you do, and you will remember more effectively everything you concentrate on.

Your mind will be like a soft, absorbent sponge and everything you concentrate on you will absorb like a sponge. When you want to remember anything you have concentrated on, you will squeeze your mind like a sponge and you will remember everything you have concentrated on.

You will feel a tremendous amount of energy with a tremendous concentration power.

You will feel a tremendous drive and concentration power with everything you do.

You have an excellent mind, and you will use it more effectively from now on every day.

Dealing with Depression

To help prevent or overcome depression, say and think these words: "Positive thoughts bring me benefits and advantages I desire."

You will direct and allow your mind to drift to positive, happy, constructive thoughts.

You will not allow anyone or anything to determine how you are going to feel. You are in control, and you choose to feel happy, important, and worthy.

You are the most important person in your world, and you will not allow anyone or anything to take that dignity away from you.

You are a fighter, and you fight for your birthright to be happy and in balance in your entire being.

CONTROLLING THE USE OF ALCOHOL

You will feel relaxed, your fingers will be relaxed, and you will not reach for alcohol to drink. You have made a decision to not drink alcohol. You will feel free of the desire to drink alcohol, and you will not drink it.

You will feel the strength to stay away from alcohol, and you will stay away from alcohol.

GAINING SOCIAL CONFIDENCE

When you see people, you will feel very talkative and very happy, and you will talk and you will smile.

You will push yourself to go out and mix socially with people. You will feel very at ease in the presence of people.

You will push yourself to meet people. You will take the initiative. You will feel the drive to go out and meet people, and you will start the conversation with ease.

You will feel the energy, drive, and desire to go out socially, and you will go out socially.

You will feel positive that everything in life will work out for you, and you will feel good about it.

You will feel confident that you are just as intelligent as anyone else and even more so. You will realize that you can talk and think just as intelligently as anyone else, and you will feel confident in all situations.

AIDING THE HEALING PROCESS

When you are injured, all you need to do to relieve the pain and promote healing is to place either hand on the injured area and say or think the word "gone," visualizing the area to be normal and healthy while healing energy from your hand penetrates the area.

You can promote healing in any area of your body by visualizing that area to be flooded in healing white light and visualizing the area to be normal and healthy.

You can help maintain and promote good health by saying and thinking these words every day: "Every day in every way I am getting better, better, and better."

When confronted with a possible illness, you can rally your body's natural powers to defeat the illness by slowly scanning your body with your visual intelligence from head to toe, pausing briefly at each portion of your body to visualize health, normality, and perfection. If your intelligence detects an abnormality, you can immediately correct it to be normal in your mind. Your body's function and balance will follow the directions you visualize and command in your mind.

You are now committing to yourself to think only positive, healthy thoughts because you know that your body will respond by being healthy and in balance.

A healthy thinking mind creates a healthy body.

IMPROVING LANGUAGE STUDY

When you study Spanish (insert other language as appropriate), *you will intensely concentrate as you study, and you will remember all the Spanish you have concentrated on.*

When you attempt to speak Spanish, all the Spanish you have studied will come to you easily and quickly, and you will speak Spanish with great ease and confidence.

You will feel a tremendous desire to learn the Spanish language, and as you study this language you will feel a tremendous concentration power, and you will remember everything you concentrate on.

INCREASING LONGEVITY

You desire a long, healthy, happy life, and your mind will direct your activities and thought patterns so you will realize this goal.

You are what you think. You are now commanding your mind to always direct you to lead your life in such a manner as to promote a long, healthy, happy life. And you will listen to and follow the beneficial dictates of your mind.

INCREASING LOVE AND TRUST

You will take people as they are. You will radiate warmth, and you will see people radiate it back.

You will feel the natural freedom to love mentally, and you will feel free of fear and free of rejection.

You will not categorize or stereotype people as being like other people you have experienced because you will realize inherently that they are not like other people.

Each person you meet is unique, and you are learning to appreciate each person as a worthwhile individual on their own merits.

IMPROVING SPEAKING SKILLS

When speaking in front of a group of people, you will intensely concentrate on your speech and you will remember easily the entire subject matter of your speech. You will speak with confidence and be free of self-consciousness.

You will speak out easily on everything you want to say in front of one person or in front of a group of people.

When you are performing in front of people, you will feel that you are performing just as well or even better than anyone else performing. You will feel free of the thought that people are just watching you. You will feel relaxed regardless of who watches.

When talking to people or in front of a group of people, you will feel a tremendous and powerful concentration power. You will remember everything with ease, and you will talk with ease. Your throat and chest will be relaxed, and you will feel free of all dryness and choking sensations.

When you speak publicly, you will feel relaxed and confident that you will sound very natural and very intelligible. You will speak with great ease.

You will feel very relaxed and yet very alert.

Every day in every way you will feel better, better, and better.

Positive thoughts bring you benefits and advantages you desire.

You are in control.

IMPROVING MONEY MANAGEMENT

You are now making a commitment to yourself to budget your money wisely by not ever allowing yourself to spend or commit to spend money you do not actually have in your possession.

You are now resolving to completely eliminate impulsive buying. You will go shopping only when you need specific items which you have listed on a paper, and you will not allow yourself to purchase any item that was not originally on your list, no matter what.

The words "bargain" and "sale" no longer entice you. You realize those words are used by someone else to get your money. You purchase only what you truly need, and you do not allow merchants to decide what you need or want.

INCREASING PHYSICAL EXERCISE

You will have the desire to physically exercise. You will find time each day to physically exercise, and you will exercise your body vigorously. And when you have done this you will feel simply great.

DEALING WITH PHOBIAS

You will feel relaxed and at ease in an airplane (insert other phobia as appropriate). You will feel relaxed, confident, and free of fear, and you will be free of fear.

STOPPING PROCRASTINATION

You will not put off doing the things you have to do. You will organize the things you have to do, and you will do them and get them out of the way.

IMPROVING READING AND STUDYING SKILLS

You will read faster and comprehend easier everything you read.

You will look forward to going to school, and you will have a serious interest in all the courses you take.

You will feel a desire to study your courses. You will concentrate tremendously on your study, and you will remember everything you concentrate on.

You will feel confident that when you take the (insert the name) exam, you will be relaxed. You will easily remember the answers you already know without tension. Right before and during the exam you will feel relaxed and confident and everything will come to you.

IMPROVING TIME MANAGEMENT

You are now making a commitment to yourself to not put off until tomorrow what can and should be done today.

You will become consciously aware every time you want to procrastinate, and you will immediately resolve not to procrastinate. You will immediately do what needs to be done.

You are becoming more conscious of time and of what you can realistically achieve in any period of time. This enables you to plan more effectively and to execute those plans more efficiently. You are becoming a better and better planner every day.

INCREASING SELF-CONFIDENCE

You will think of the present and future only.

It will be so easy for you to achieve the success and happiness you want and deserve. For you are the product of your own thought patterns. Think success, and you are a success. Think beauty, and you are beautiful. Think strength, and you are strong. Think positively and constructively, and your life becomes a positive and constructive experience. These things are your new image...the new you...stronger and stronger every day.

You are now learning to be in total control of every aspect of your life. You will always be relaxed and calm and in control. No longer will you allow others to exercise control over you. You are in control.

You are a beautiful, intelligent, and worthwhile person. And every day from now on you will become more completely the person you really want to be. You will be confident, relaxed, poised, charming, optimistic, and firm in your resolution to do what you want for your own happiness.

Never again will you be a slave to anything, to any person, or to any job. You are your own person, and you are in total control.

IMPROVING SEXUAL PERFORMANCE, FEMALE SUBJECT

When you have sexual relations, you will feel relaxed and you will reach a climax.

You will feel a natural physical attraction toward the opposite sex.

When you have sexual relations, you will not block. You will not fear failure. You will feel positive and confident that you will have an orgasm, and you will naturally have an orgasm.

When you have sexual relations with a man, you will feel tremendous physical desire for him. When you feel him penetrate your body, you will experience heightened excitement and enjoyment, and will have multiple orgasms during the entire lovemaking period.

NOTE: The following two suggestions are especially helpful for frigidity.

You will always find that the touch and sight of your male companion is exciting and sexually stimulating. Even the slightest physical contact with your love companion will cause you to desire sexual relations, and you will reach a climax and have multiple orgasms.

Every day your sexual appetite will be stronger and stronger, and you will feel better and better. You will find yourself becoming more and more sexually responsive to your love partner by easily becoming aroused and experiencing orgasms.

IMPROVING SEXUAL PERFORMANCE, MALE SUBJECT

When you have sexual relations, you will feel relaxed and you will achieve erection and ejaculation.

You will feel a natural physical attraction toward the opposite sex.

When you have sexual relations, you will not block. You will not fear failure. You will feel positive and confident that you will have a firm, lasting erection and have a satisfying ejaculation.

Whenever you have sexual relations with a woman, you will have a powerful ejaculation and a complete release of semen.

When you have sexual relations with a woman, you will feel a tremendous physical desire for her. When you penetrate this woman you will have a very stiff, rigid erection. You will maintain this erection until the woman has climaxed, and only then will you have an ejaculation.

When you have physical relations with a woman, you will have a very stiff, rigid erection. You will feel great pleasure, and it will feel good.

NOTE: The following two suggestions are especially helpful for impotence.

You will always find that the touch and sight of a female companion is sexually stimulating. Even the slightest physical contact with a consenting woman will cause you to desire sexual relations, and your penis will become firm and erect.

Every day your sexual appetite will be stronger and stronger, and you will feel better and better. You will find yourself becoming more and more sexually responsive to your love partner by easily getting and maintaining a rigid erection.

IMPROVING SLEEPING HABITS

When you go to sleep this evening, you will quickly drop off into a deep, sound sleep for eight hours. The next thing you know, it will be daylight, and you will awaken refreshed and alert.

QUITTING SMOKING

Regardless of what happens at work, you will feel relaxed. You will feel free of the desire to smoke the entire working time.

You are in total control of every aspect of your life. Cigarettes no longer have any part in your life. You are now a non-smoker. You will remain a non-smoker the rest of your life. You have made this healthy decision, and you are happy with that decision. You are in control. Cigarettes have no control over you any longer. You have resolved to break the bad habit of smoking, and you have broken that bad habit.

CONTROLLING WEIGHT

You will feel satisfied with very small quantities of food, and these small quantities of food will satisfy you completely.

You will feel the strength to stay away from, and you will stay away from unhealthy foods such as sweets and starches.

You will have no desire to eat anything between meals or after dinner at night. After dinner, you will have no desire to eat anything until breakfast tomorrow morning.

All the calories in the foods you eat will be completely utilized by your body and not stored as unnecessary fat.

You will strictly follow the diet you prescribe for yourself, eating nothing between meals or after dinner. You will eat only the foods prescribed by your diet, and when you have done this you will no longer feel hungry.

IMPROVING WORK SUCCESS

You will handle all situations on the job in a very relaxed, calm, and sensible manner free of tension.

During your working hours you will feel relaxed and calm. Regardless of what happens, you will handle every situation in a relaxed, calm, and sensible manner free of tension.

You will make decisions on the job, and you will feel great confidence in your decisions.

In your working hours on the job, you will feel a powerful and intense concentration power on your work. You will work very, very fast with a tremendous amount of energy.

You will look forward to the job interview. You will feel completely at ease during job interviews. You will feel confident that you will radiate all the personable and knowledgeable qualities and work interest that the employer seeks. You will speak in a calm, concise, and meaningful manner without tension.

You will feel an intense interest in your work, and you will feel a tremendous drive to perform to the best of your ability.

You are a successful person, and you enjoy your success. Part of your success is your ability to manage your time efficiently. You plan your time and your projects, and you execute your plan promptly without allowing yourself to be distracted.

You will provide honest and sincere service for your customers, knowing that your rewards will follow as a result.

You are capable and efficient, and your creative mind knows what you can do. Your creative mind will find a way to lead you into the right circumstances and situations to best take advantage of your abilities.

You are learning to relax...to release all anxiety and relax and let go. For you are in control of all aspects of your life now. No longer will you allow anxiety, tension, or nervous energy to impede you. Every day you will notice yourself relaxing more. You will notice yourself becoming more calm and more in control than ever before.

You will notice every day that your attitude is becoming more and more philosophical and free of serious concern about life's daily problems.

You are an excellent salesperson, and each day you will feel yourself becoming even more successful as the new, confident, relaxed YOU becomes more and more prominent in your personality.

CHAPTER 10

Other Kinds of Hypnosis

HYPNOSIS FOR CHILDREN

The techniques and routines covered thus far in this book are for adults. Specifically for about ages fourteen and up. Children, however, don't need such lengthy procedures because their brain activity is already predominantly in alpha. It is much easier and faster to induce hypnosis in children; the younger they are, the faster they respond, and the shorter the procedure needed. Also, their attention span is such that they won't listen to a lot of boring words. Hypnosis for children often makes use of physical contact.

Children's minds are very powerful because they don't clutter up their beliefs with all of the artificial and false nonsense that most adults do. They have not yet acquired the inhibitions and artificial barriers in their thinking and behavior that most adults have. As a result, children respond to hypnotic suggestions easily, quickly, and very effectively. It takes longer to condition adults—to bypass their inhibitions—and reach the child within. Children think, "I can." Most adults tend to think, "I can't." As the Roman poet Virgil wrote over 2,000 years ago, "They can because they think they can."

Case History

Eleven-year-old Mary (not her real name) had been experiencing a constant earache in her left ear for many days due to a severe infection. Her physician had given her medication for the infection, but it was working very slowly. The pain relievers were not working at all.

My wife and I were visiting Mary's parents at the time, and I asked the parents if they would allow me to hypnotize Mary to alleviate her pain. They agreed.

I had Mary stand in front of me with her left ear facing me.

"What is your problem?" I asked

She replied tearfully, "My ear hurts."

"Do you want it to hurt?"

"No."

"Would you like me to take away the pain?"

She nodded yes.

"Close your eyes, Mary. I am putting my hand by your ear about a quarter inch away. Do you feel the warmth of my hand?" (I had the palm of my right hand covering her left ear, not touching it, about one quarter inch away).

"Yes."

"Good. Now I want you to imagine that you have an eye inside you that can go anywhere inside your body and look at things. Can you do that?"

"Yes."

"Good. Now look inside your left ear with that eye where you feel the warmth of my hand. Can you see the inside of your ear?"

"Yes."

"Very good. Now imagine strong energy coming from my hand into your ear. This energy will help you. Now I want you to light up the inside of your ear with your own energy. It will be like turning on a light in a dark cave. Light up your ear with the energy. This is your healing energy which takes away all pain and causes the ear to get well. Have you done this?"

"Yes." She began smiling.

"Mary, I am going to count from 1 to 3 and snap my fingers. When I do, you will open your eyes and your ear will feel fine, and it will continue to feel fine. 1...2...3. Open eyes and feeling fine."

She opened her eyes and smiled. "Thank you," she said. The pain was gone and she ran off to play.

This entire procedure lasted about two minutes. I merely directed the child's tremendous creative ability to bring about results. By the way, the infection rapidly cleared up and was gone in another twenty-four hours.

Make a strong mental note of several important points concerning the techniques in this case. First, I asked Mary what was wrong. Although I knew what was wrong, I wanted her to define the problem and thus focus her attention on it. Second, I asked if she wanted the problem. Again, I knew the answer, but by her saying no, she made a commitment to herself to get rid of the problem. Third, I asked if she wanted my help. Her yes answer solidified her commitment and put her faith in me and in what I was going to do. At this point, the problem was already half solved. From that point on, I utilized and directed her own creative energies to solve the rest of the problem.

Children's Routine 1

This routine is especially effective for ages five to eight years old. The brain activity in children this age is almost exclusively in alpha so hypnosis and suggestion are very quickly effective. The induction procedure is almost entirely a physical, rather than verbal, procedure. The suggestions are brief and to the point. Typically this entire procedure won't last more than two minutes. You can use this procedure for almost any purpose from stopping bed-wetting to coping with a fear of the dark.

I also use this quick routine on adults whom I have previously hypnotized and on those who have a short attention span due to some sort of infirmity. Quick routines are also excellent for relieving pain or anxiety in an emergency situation.

Have the child stand straight against a wall with feet together and heels against the wall. Place a chair for yourself about 2 feet in front of the child and sit in it, facing the child. Instruct the child as follows:

Tommy, when I tell you, I want you to start bending over. You will soon lose your balance and start to fall forward, and I will catch you.

At this point, extend your arms and keep them extended to show the child you can and will catch him.

When you feel yourself fall into my arms, just close your eyes and rest in my arms while I talk to you for just a short time. Do you understand?

If he doesn't understand, explain until he does, then proceed.

All right, Tommy, start to bend over now. Keep bending until you fall into my arms.

When he falls into your arms say:

Close your eyes and just rest here in my arms for a short time while I talk to you.

At this point you give the suggestions. For example:

Tiny babies wet the bed because they are so small they are not able to go to the bathroom. Big people do not wet the bed because they know how to go to the bathroom anytime they want to. You are a big person, Tommy, and you get bigger every day. You know how to go to the bathroom all by yourself because you are big. From now on you will always go to the bathroom whenever you need to go. Even if you are sleeping in bed, you will wake up if you need to go to the bathroom, and you will get up and go to the bathroom as soon as you wake up. You will not wet the bed anymore because you now know how to wake up and go to the bathroom by yourself. You will feel good every time you get up and go to the bathroom instead of wetting the bed.

I am now going to stand you up and you can open your eyes and be wide awake.

Gently stand the child upright and say:

Open eyes! Wide awake and feeling fine!

It is not unusual for the child to ask to go to the bathroom immediately upon awakening from this brief hypnosis session. When he does, it immediately reinforces the suggestion.

Following is a brief analysis of the salient points of this procedure.

The induction gains the child's trust. Every child knows he can easily bend over without losing his balance. Yet when you tell him to bend, he does lose his balance and falls into your arms just as you said he would. This immediately establishes his confidence and trust in you because it happened just as you said it would even though he doesn't know why. The reason why (which you do not explain) is that it is impossible for anyone to stand flush against a wall with feet together and then bend over without falling. This is because when a person bends, the buttocks push against the wall, thrusting the body forward and off balance. This is why the procedure is good for younger children but not for older ones who could easily figure it out.

You hold the child in your arms. This establishes contact and rapport. Also the child is in a physical position that keeps him from fidgeting or engaging in any sort of physical distraction.

The suggestion is brief, logical, and to the point. It should always be a positive suggestion that makes the child feel good about himself. The example given capitalizes on every child's desire to be big and achieve goals that big people achieve.

The wake up is simple and quick. The subject knows that when you have assisted him to his feet and let him go, it is all over and he is in charge again.

Children's Routine 2

This routine is excellent for all ages from five to a hundred. I especially like it for children from about nine to fourteen. This procedure also utilizes some physical positioning and physical contact with a minimum of verbal speaking. The entire procedure will last about five to seven minutes, depending on the extent of your suggestions.

Seat the child in a straight-back, armless chair positioned so no harsh light falls on her eyes. Have her rest her arms in her lap. Feet flat on the floor and slightly apart. Stand immediately in front of her, slightly to her right. A good way to position yourself is to have your right foot between her two feet, but not touching. This puts your right eye in approximately the same vertical plane as her right eye.

Have her gaze straight ahead. This brings her line of vision about at your waist or chest, depending on your height and hers.

Put the tip of your right index finger on your own right cheekbone just under your right eye and say:

Karen (substitute child's name), *I want you to keep your head facing straight ahead. Just roll your eyes upward to focus your gaze on my right finger which I am holding beneath my right eye.*

In a moment I am going to slowly move my finger from my cheek, through the air, and touch your forehead. I want you to follow the movement of my finger with your eyes until I touch your forehead. When you feel my finger touch your forehead, I want you to close your eyes, take a deep breath, and relax. Now watch my finger.

Start moving your finger slowly from your cheek, through the air toward her forehead. Take 5 to 10 seconds to do this to allow her plenty of eye concentration and strain.

When you touch her forehead say:

Eyes closed! Take a deep breath, and relax.

Remove your finger from her forehead.

Allow your head to droop slightly as all your neck muscles relax. Feel this relaxation flow up into your face and eyes, a warm tingling feeling. Allow this relaxation to flow downward throughout your entire body now. Feel the warm, tingling relaxation go into your shoulders, your chest, waist, hips, thighs, calves, ankles, feet, and toes. Completely relaxed from head to toes.

In a moment, I am going to gently pick up each of your hands, one at a time, and let them drop back onto your lap. Each time I do, you will relax even more completely.

Using your right thumb and forefinger, gently grasp her right wrist and raise her hand about 2 inches from her lap, then release your grip allowing the hand to flop back onto her lap. Say: Relax at the moment you drop the hand. Do this three times with her right hand and three times with her left hand.

At this point you give the suggestions. For example:

I want you to imagine now that you are in school at your desk taking your spelling exam. You are relaxed and confident. You are intelligent and you have a perfect memory. You can easily remember anything you have studied. See your teacher standing in front of the class. She pronounces the first spelling word. You quickly write the word on your paper. You have spelled it correctly. The teacher pronounces word after word after word, and you easily write them all down correctly. It feels so good to you. You notice that some other children seem to be having problems, but you do not have a problem because you have learned to relax and let your excellent mind easily do the work for you. And tomorrow when you take your spelling exam you will be just as relaxed as you are now and your mind will work easily and correctly to furnish you all the information you need to spell all the words correctly. You are a bright, capable person in everything you put your mind to do.

Now I am going to count from 1 to 3 and snap my fingers. When I snap my fingers you will open your eyes, be wide awake, feeling fine and full of mental energy and confidence. 1...2...3.

(Snap.)

Open eyes! Wide awake and full of energy and confidence.

Following is a brief analysis of the salient points of this procedure:

The physical positioning is very important. Stand in front of the subject so she must look up to you. This puts you in an authoritative position in her eyes so she will automatically follow your direction without question. However, you stand slightly to one side so as not to completely block her. This keeps her from becoming intimidated or apprehensive.

The finger to forehead movement causes the subject's eyes to roll upward and become slightly tired or strained. This action automatically triggers the alpha level of brain activity.

You use a quick physical relaxation procedure. This procedure is reinforced and deepened by the hand dropping routine.

This procedure is somewhere between the young children's procedure and the full adult procedure. It is a very effective procedure for all ages. I use it frequently.

Summary

Hypnosis procedures for children are short and fast. Usually the procedures involve a liberal use of physical activity or contact to implement the induction. The suggestions need to be carefully structured to get the message across completely and quickly in an upbeat manner. The two procedures detailed here are two I use often, but by no means are these the only ones. These examples provide you with a good start.

Very little, if any, pre-hypnosis counseling is needed with children because they don't need it. Their minds are not cluttered with erroneous pre-conceived ideas like most adults' minds are. Children accept things as they are and respond accordingly. In many ways, they are more adult than adults, so treat them that way. Here's an ironclad rule to remember when dealing with children: Never talk down to them or treat them in a condescending manner. They are every bit your equal and deserve to be treated respectfully and equally.

One Caution: Never, never hypnotize a child without parental permission, and always have at least one parent present during the entire hypnosis session. If you can have both parents, or two adults the child knows and trusts, so much the better. This is to protect the child and make him more comfortable. And it is to protect you from false accusations or possible lawsuits.

Burn it into your mind: NEVER without permission and ALWAYS with responsible adult witnesses.

GROUP HYPNOSIS

There may be times when you are asked to speak to a high school or college class, a club or other organization, or even an informal house party. In these group situations, make the highlight of your presentation a brief deep-relaxation session for the entire group. With group hypnosis, use the same routines as for an individual. Because you are not interested in solving specific problems, use a few routines that will provide a light hypnosis, put in a few generic suggestions, and then bring out the subjects.

Pre-Hypnosis Instructions

Before you begin the demonstration, talk to the group about hypnosis. In addition, I suggest laying two ground rules. First, there is to be no smoking in the room prior to the start of the lecture or during the lecture and demonstration. (I also do not allow smoking in the room where I do individual hypnosis sessions.) In other words, there must be no presence of smoke—

not even residual smoke. The reason is that in the altered state of consciousness, people become hypersensitive and smoke, even from one cigarette, can trigger severe coughing in some people.

Second, instruct the group that if anyone chooses not to participate, that is fine. They can sit with their eyes open and watch or leave the room. Ask that they not disturb those who are participating. Tell those who are participating that if they want to, they can open their eyes and take a peek at what is going on. Stress that this is just a mini-demonstration of deep relaxation techniques. When group members know they can choose and peek, they become more comfortable and allay any apprehensions. (I have never yet had anyone who wouldn't participate or who opened their eyes to peek.)

The Demonstration Routine

Begin the session with routines A, B, C, F, G, I or whatever other arrangement you prefer. (Routines A and B are found in chapter 2, Routines C, F, G, and I are found in chapter 3.) Then give some generic suggestions such as:

You are now in a very healthy, relaxed state and you can use this state to achieve any worthwhile goal.

You are a good, worthy person and every day you will learn more about using your mind and skills in a beneficial way.

You are a successful person and you enjoy your success.

I will stop talking now for thirty seconds to give you time to program your own individual goal.

(Stop talking and time the thirty seconds on your watch). When the time is up, bring them out using a routine similar to routine Q (found in chapter 3).

Close with a question and answer dialog about the experience. You can usually get this going by asking, "Tell me about your experience." If there is reluctance to speak first, pick out someone and say, "How about you, Diane. Did you relax? Did you have a goal that you programmed?"

STAGE HYPNOSIS

The stage hypnotist is a performer who is also a very good hypnotist. His purpose is to entertain, and he does so by selecting subjects from the audience who are good hypnosis subjects and then has those subjects perform funny or incredible acts while under light hypnosis.

In the beginning he doesn't know who in the audience is a good subject, but he knows that statistically there are three or four in any group of a dozen he could pick. So he invites a dozen volunteers onto the stage. People who volunteer tend to be uninhibited and freewheeling—something the hypnotist is looking for.

He uses a few quick routines on his dozen volunteers and observes them carefully. Because he knows people and his trade, it is easy for him to spot those who will give him problems; he either asks those subjects to return to the audience or he leaves them on stage but doesn't use them.

Moving quickly, he concentrates on the subjects he knows are likely to respond well. He uses quick routines to induce light hypnosis and directs the subjects to perform entertaining acts. For example, he might get a man to give a stirring speech on behalf of women's liberation or ask a subject to bark like a dog. The repertoire can be nearly limitless.

In many stage demonstrations, the hypnotist tells his subjects, "When you awaken you will not remember anything that happened while you were hypnotized." Since a hypnotized person always remembers unless he is told he won't, the stage hypnotist probably says this so the subject won't feel embarrassed afterward.

Most stage hypnotists are skilled, sensitive to their subjects, and use safe methods. A clumsy or careless hypnotist, however, could potentially do harm to his subjects.

I have not done stage hypnosis and do not intend to. To me, hypnosis is a valuable tool for helping people enrich their lives. Good stage hypnotists are somewhat like great brain surgeons who restrict their practice to removing skin warts. There is nothing wrong with removing skin warts, but what a waste of skill. Perhaps some stage hypnotists earn their living on the stage but use their skills off stage to help people.

CHAPTER 11

Additional Case Histories

Throughout this book, you've read case histories to illustrate certain points and techniques. In this chapter, you'll find a few more brief profiles to give you an even broader perspective of the uses of hypnosis (I picked some of the more interesting cases to include here). Although these cases don't even scratch the surface as far as what you can do with hypnosis, you'll find sufficient examples to give you an idea of situations you may encounter and how you might handle them.

In addition to diet control, regression, and other instances mentioned in this book, other cases that have been handled using hypnosis include:

- coping with fears and phobias (including fear of death, fear of failure, fear of flying, and fear of inadequacy)

- coping with guilt (including guilt about cheating, lying, and having an abortion)

- improving test taking and memory skills

- controlling suicidal feelings

- controlling habits (including nail biting and excessive use of alcohol)
- controlling stress
- improving self-image and self-confidence
- controlling migraines, aches and pains, illnesses
- enhancing skills
- dealing with sexual problems (including impotency), lack of energy, insomnia

A Test-Taking Case

When my youngest daughter, Eileen, was fifteen, she took a typing course in high school. In order to get an A in the course, she had to type 45 words per minute. She could type even faster than that when not under pressure, but she froze up on tests. The very word "test" caused her brain and fingers to go out to lunch.

The night before her big test, I hypnotized her. Under hypnosis I had her visualize herself typing at lightning speeds with no errors, all the while feeling calm, at ease, and in total control. Then I gave her the post-hypnotic suggestion that she would type 45 words per minute the next day on her typing test and that she would remain relaxed throughout the entire test.

She typed exactly 45 words per minute on the test and earned her A. She reported feeling relaxed and confident throughout the test.

Notice that hypnosis did not enable Eileen to do something she wasn't normally capable of. She had the capability but had been putting obstacles in her path.

Hypnosis removed those obstacles, allowing her to express her ability. She typed exactly 45 words per minute because that is what I had told her to do under hypnosis. If I had said 50 words, she would have done that because that was still in her ability range. If I had said 200 words per minute, she would not have done it because that was beyond her ability, but she would have tried to do it. If I had said 200 words a minute, my guess is that the effort and resulting failure could have introduced another problem and frustration. So be careful of what you suggest to your subjects. You want to enable them and improve them, not introduce additional problems.

An Insomnia Case

An elderly woman came in for a free consultation to ask about my fees and if I could help her overcome her insomnia. Typically, she lay awake nearly all night, every night, not getting her needed rest. She was on social security and couldn't afford a multi-session program. She felt all she could afford was one $25 session.

"Couldn't you help me in just one session?" she pleaded.

I have a special place in my heart for the elderly so I said confidently, "Yes, I can!" Although at that moment I didn't have any idea of how I was going to do it.

I quickly altered my own state of consciousness and mentally said, "Help!" to my own higher mind. I immediately got the awareness I needed to proceed.

In response to my questioning, she told me she could borrow her son's tape recorder. So I turned on my tape recorder and took her into deep relaxation. My suggestions incorporated these key elements:

That she would drift into a deep, completely restful, natural sleep and remain soundly asleep until it was time for her to awaken.

That she would awaken whenever she heard my voice directing her to do so, or whenever any emergency situation arose that required her to be wide awake and alert, or whenever she had had her full complement of needed sleep, or whenever her pre-set alarm clock went off.

That regardless of the amount of time she slept, she would always awaken feeling completely rested and full of energy as though she had eight full hours of perfect, relaxing sleep.

That she would listen to this tape recording every night for thirty days, and it would always put her into perfect, restful sleep right away.

That at the end of thirty days her mind would be completely trained, and she was to discontinue using the tape recording.

I turned off the tape recorder and allowed her to continue to sleep in my office for another fifteen minutes. After fifteen minutes, I awakened her. I did not turn on the tape recorder for the awakening process because I wanted a tape to put her to sleep, not awaken her. She awakened completely refreshed and alert. I gave her the tape, and she went home.

A month later, she called to tell me that she was now off the tape and sleeping well naturally every night. It worked!

This case illustrates several interesting points, including how to improvise on the spur of the moment and use your own altered state of consciousness to obtain the information you need. I use my own altered state many times every day to tap into my own higher mind for greater awareness. You, too, can develop this ability.

A Prostitute Case

A prostitute wanted to give up her profession and get married. She had fallen in love and wanted to become an average housewife and ultimately a mother. Her problem was that she did not enjoy sex. In her entire life she had never experienced an orgasm. Sex was just a mechanical skill for her to use to get whatever she wanted. Now she wanted to change all that. She wanted to experience the enjoyment, but she didn't know how to allow that to happen.

This was a difficult case because I had to deal with many issues, including poor self-image, negative feelings toward men in general, and fear of releasing her toughness and allowing her femininity to emerge.

She prepaid for six session and I outlined two main purposes for each session. First, I wanted to deal with the many issues. Second, I wanted her to visualize performing sexual acts where she would experience pleasure and satisfaction.

During session 1, I had her commit to herself to have sexual relations only with the man she loved.

Insofar as I know, this suggestion was immediately successful. Her visualization of pleasurable sex, however, did not appear to be successful.

A week later at the start of session 2, she reported having had sexual relations every day with her lover, but there had been no enjoyment. During hypnosis, her visualization appeared to produce some physical excitement during mental sex.

Next week at the start of session 3, she reported no pleasure with actual sexual relations. During session 3, her visualization caused a very strong orgasm. She called me the next morning to say that after session 3 she went to her lover and experienced the most profound physical pleasure imaginable.

I never saw or heard from her after that. She didn't return for her remaining three sessions or request a refund for the unused sessions. I couldn't get in touch with her because she had refused to give me an address or phone number where she could be reached. I hope the story had a happy ending.

A Tennis Case

A professional tennis player hit a performance slump and couldn't snap herself out of it. Each time she lost, she sunk into deeper depression. She now expected herself to lose—and she did. Even players who were far below her skill beat her. She was the tennis pro at a posh country club, and now was in danger of losing her job because of her constant "duffer" performance. Her serve had become weak, her returns went into the net, she was always in the wrong position and off balance, she had little zip and energy, her moves were sluggish, and her timing was off.

I saw her for the first time in a morning appointment. She had a game scheduled that afternoon with a mediocre player. She was sure she would be fired if she lost.

Under hypnosis I had her visualize a perfect tennis game where her timing was perfect, her serve deadly and full of fire, and her movements agile and quick. I had her visualize anticipating her opponent's every action and being in exactly the right position. She visualized a game where she did everything right and won without her opponent even scoring one point.

That afternoon she won—just barely—but she won for the first time in many weeks of daily play.

After four hypnosis sessions, she was once again soundly beating everyone in sight so there was no need to continue the sessions. She had quickly mastered her self-hypnosis, and I am confident that she will never again experience a slump in performance.

AN ABORTION CASE

A psychiatric nurse brought her fourteen-year-old daughter to me because the girl was experiencing severe guilt feelings over having had a recent abortion. She had become depressed and withdrawn. She had no faith in herself or in anyone. The boy who had impregnated her deserted her once she became pregnant. Other boys now considered her as an easy score and tried to seduce her.

In reality, she was a lovely, good, worthy young woman who had made one error with a boy under the delusion that she was in love. She didn't deserve this continued punishment she was experiencing.

My job was to get her to forgive herself and all others and rebuild her self-image. For the most part, I used the standard techniques found in this book and was successful.

The one thing I did in this case that I want to highlight is the use of the Seashore Trip Routine (found in chapter 12). In the Seashore Trip, I had her do four things while she was standing in the sand near the water's edge.

First, I had her write in the sand "I forgive" and then write her own name, the name of her ex-boyfriend, the names of any others who she had felt bitterness toward, and "all others." Then I had her visualize a wave sweeping up over her feet and over the forgiveness message she had written in the sand. When the wave receded, the sand was once again smooth, the message was gone. The message had been carried out into the sea of life where it became a reality. All was truly forgiven.

Second, I had her write "I love" in the sand followed by her own name, any special names she chose, and "all others." Once again the wave took the message out into the sea of life. Her love was truly a reality.

Third, I had her stand on the beach facing the sea. I had her turn to her right and notice an open door on the beach. I told her that to the right was the past, and this was the door to the past. I had her walk over to the door, close it and lock it, and throw the key into the sea. She had now closed the door on the past and could no longer be negatively influenced by the past.

Fourth, I had her turn and go to the left up the beach where there was a closed door standing. I told her that to the left was the future, and this was the door to the future. I had her unlock the door, open it, and put the key in her pocket. I had her gaze through the open door and see herself beautiful, relaxed, mature, peaceful, and extremely happy. This was her future and she owned the key to it.

This kind of session is extremely powerful and good. Realize that I have provided just the outline. You will need to supply the specific set of words to perform this session.

A Cut Chin Case

In this case, I was both the operator and the subject. It illustrates how self-hypnosis can be valuable in an emergency.

My wife and I were vacationing at a lake one summer, spending most of our time out on our 18-foot power cruiser. This particular day we had been lying at anchor, and I walked out onto the bow to pull in the anchor so we could get underway. I slipped on the bow and fell, hitting the point of my chin hard on the metal bow rail. When I pulled myself up into a sitting position, blood poured down my chest from my chin.

My wife's face was ashen. "My God!" she screamed. "I can see the bone."

I immediately pinched the wound shut as hard as I could. As I sat there on the bow, I closed my eyes and almost instantly altered my state of consciousness (in retrospect, I think I probably went all the way down into theta).

I visualized my chin in perfect condition. I bathed it in white healing light and mentally said, "No bleeding. No pain. No scar. No infection. No swelling. Just perfect healing at one thousand times my normal healing rate." I sat there for five minutes, pinching the wound shut, while I remained in an altered state with eyes closed. I maintained the vision of a perfect chin while mentally repeating the words several more times.

Then I brought myself out and opened my eyes. I stopped pinching the wound. There was no more bleeding. A blood scab had formed. It didn't hurt. My wife wanted to return to shore to cleanse and dress my chin. I said no, I was all right. We got underway and enjoyed several hours of boating before going ashore.

When I awakened the next morning I found that the blood scab had come off during the night. The only reminder of the accident was a thin, red pencil-like line about an inch long on my chin. Within a week, even this pencil line was completely gone. No evidence of the accident was left. And at no time was there pain or swelling.

A MEMORY CASE

A man called me for an appointment to begin a series of sessions for memory improvement. He said he had acute memory failure. Of course, he forgot to show up for his appointment. He phoned again and made another appointment. Again he forgot. This went on for four consecutive appointments. I knew if I could get him into the office just once, I could give him a post-hypnotic suggestion to return the following week and eventually get him to solve his problem.

So when he phoned again, I had him immediately write a note to remind him of the appointment which I made for 9 A.M. the following morning. I told him to tape it on the glass of the rear view mirror of his car. I stayed on the phone while he did that and returned to confirm to me that he had done it.

This time he showed up for the appointment. After six sessions, for which he was always on time, he had a marvelous memory.

A CUT FOOT CASE

Some years ago when I had just begun to practice hypnosis professionally, a young woman came in for her appointment on crutches and wearing a cast on her lower left leg and foot. A couple of days before, she ran barefoot in her yard and stepped on something that lacerated the bottom of her foot to the bone from toe to heel. She told me how many stitches the doctor had to put in and that he told her she would be in the cast for at least three weeks and perhaps longer. The doctor had also said she probably wouldn't be able to wear a shoe on that foot for several more weeks after the cast was removed.

She was coming to me for diet control, so I hypnotized her and performed the diet control suggestions.

She was one of the most receptive hypnosis subjects I have ever had; I could practically hypnotize her by just saying "Close your eyes and relax." She responded marvelously.

Before I brought her out, I took her through a procedure and suggestions similar to what I had done to myself when I had cut my chin.

The next week she returned for her next appointment without crutches, without a cast on her leg, and wearing high-heeled shoes. She took off her left shoe to show me the bottom of her foot. There was a thin, red line from toe to heel and that was all. No swelling or discoloration. The wound had healed.

This story has a punch line, and she was bursting to tell me. It seems she had gone to her doctor the day after the hypnosis session and insisted that he remove the cast. He refused, and a heated argument ensued. She vowed to take a hammer and break it off herself. To save her potential injury from doing it herself, the doctor reluctantly removed the cast, but he warned her it was at her own risk and was going to cost her more money. She said the look on his face was priceless when he saw a healed foot.

"I don't understand," he muttered.

Then the young woman told him about the hypnosis session.

The doctor became furious. "I thought you had more sense than to go to quacks!" he scolded. "Obviously, you don't trust me to be your physician. Consider this your last visit to my office. Find yourself another doctor, or should I say find a quack!"

Unruffled, the young woman asked, "Doctor, how do you explain the healing?"

"Obviously, I misdiagnosed it!" he snorted, leaving the examining room.

I've often wondered how you can misdiagnose a lacerated foot.

This case illustrates the blind, fanatical opposition that exists against hypnosis. People tend to oppose anything they do not understand.

Our role as hypnotists is not to meet these opponents in head to head confrontation, but rather to provide patient, knowledgeable education about hypnosis. And most importantly of all, provide our services with integrity, honesty, and sensitivity. First learn your skill well, then practice it with honor.

Chapter 12

Additional Routines

In this chapter, you'll find a few more routines to augment the ones found in other chapters. Although the routines described here are more specialized, you can easily fit them into a set of standard routines to achieve a specific purpose.

Seashore Trip Routine

This routine is one of the most effective; it is flexible and used for an endless list of situations. Modified versions of this routine appear in chapters 7, 8, and 11. You can also use this routine in place of the Mountain Trip routine in session 6 (see chapter 6).

Picture yourself sitting on a large rock outcropping with the sea about 20 feet below...notice the roar as the ocean rushes in and hits the rocks below us...smell the salt air as the wind gushes against our face...notice the contrast between our rocks and the beach.

Notice the sea gulls in the sky above...watch them dive for their dinner in the sea below...listen to their chatter as they return to the sky...notice the other birds around us...they show their appreciation for life in their smooth gliding and happy song.

Look behind us and we see a trail to our beach ...let's walk down that trail to our beach below...the smooth path seems to indicate how many people have climbed down from our rock before us...these ageless rocks seem to reassure us of the beauty of life, and how being in harmony with nature seems to give us grace ...the stones and rocks seem to make a slight set of natural stairs about halfway down...now back to the sloping trail...the sand is warming up and is so inviting...let's take off our shoes and finish our walk to the beach barefooted...feel the warm sand squish up between our toes...feel the breeze warm us as we reach the beach...we are now able to look over the calm sea, glistening to our eyes.

Let's walk toward the water...feel the difference of the wet sand from the dry sand we just left...bend down and write "I love you"...and then put the names of our special people we wish to remember...now see the sea rush past us, give our ankles a hug, and as it returns, takes our names and our message "I love you."

Since the hug from the sea felt so good as it took our names and message, bend down again and write "I love you"...and then put the names of the people you feel you have slighted or hurt...now see the wave rush past us, give your ankles a big hug, and as it returns, takes our names and our message, "I love you."

Walk further into the ocean to where the water is about up to your knees and feel the cool reassurance of life...now draw in the love of life from this sea...up through your feet, until it fills your whole body with excitement and love of life.

Now let's return to the beach...pick up that sea-shell...listen to the message from the shell...back on the warm sand...turn and look at the sea once more and say "good-bye"...it is time for us to return to our shoes...and back up the stairs of life...to the top of the rock. We have the love and excitement of life drawn up from the sea within us now...say a special thanks to those people who have been thoughtful to you as your sea fades from view.

BALLOON COUNTDOWN

This routine is nice for group hypnosis, or you can use it for one person with slight modification. This also is a good routine for children.

Stretch your right arm and left leg and relax. Now stretch your left arm and right leg and relax. Now stretch both arms and both legs...all over...and relax. Flop your arms and legs into a lazy, comfortable position and close your eyes.

To take a balloon breath, you breathe in through your nose and see a balloon coming toward you. To blow out a balloon breath, you blow out through your mouth and blow the balloon away. And when you get to your favorite place, remember to be very still and quiet.

Now see before you a red balloon. Take a balloon breath; see the red balloon come toward you. Now blow the red balloon away.

See before you an orange balloon. Take a balloon breath; see the orange balloon come toward you. Now blow the orange balloon away.

See a yellow balloon. Take a balloon breath and see the yellow balloon come toward you. Now blow the yellow balloon away.

See a green balloon. Take a balloon breath and see the green balloon come toward you. Now blow the green balloon away.

See a blue balloon. Take a balloon breath and see the blue balloon come toward you. Now blow the blue balloon away.

Now breathe in and see 10. Hold the breath and see 9. Breathe out and see 8. Breathe in and see 7. Hold the breath and see 6. Breathe out and see 5. Breathe in and see 4. Hold the breath and see 3. Breathe out and see 2.

Now see a large number 1 tied to a purple balloon. Grab hold of the number 1 and blow yourself away to your favorite place. Your favorite place can be anywhere you want. It can have anything you want in it, because it is your place, your very own place.

(Wait for 30 seconds to a minute to allow the subjects to create their favorite place and to explore it. Then continue.)

Take a balloon breath and you will feel better. You will relax more in your favorite place. When you want to remember something, take a balloon breath and see the answer behind your eyes. To be in charge of yourself, take a balloon breath. You will do whatever you believe you can do. Give yourself a hug with your elbows for being special people. Now send a mental message to someone special.

(At this point put in whatever suggestions are appropriate for the work you are doing.)

To return from your favorite place, take a balloon breath. See a white balloon with your favorite color stripes on it. Hold onto the striped balloon and blow yourself back. Now everyone open eyes. Stretch. Feeling fine.

TEST TAKING

You will be especially calm, relaxed, and confident every time you take a test or examination of any kind. And your brain and eyes will function perfectly when taking any test or exam. Here is how to get an excellent score on every test you take:

First, read the question and answer it if you immediately know the correct answer; if not, do not spend time on it, just go on to the next question. Continue with this method until you have quickly gone over every question on the test once. At this point you will have answered some of the questions...just the ones that you immediately knew the correct answer to.

Second, go over each question you didn't answer the first time. Spend a little more time on each question, about one minute...no longer. Answer the ones for which an answer comes to mind, then go on to the next question. Continue this way until you have gone over the questions you missed the first time through. You will find that you have picked up a few more answers.

Third, go to any questions that may be still unanswered and mentally ask the teacher for the answer and write down the first thing that comes into your mind. Do this for each remaining unanswered question. This way you will turn in a completed paper and will have a good score.

MIGRAINES

In pre-hypnosis instructions, tell your subject to use her self-hypnosis when she feels the first symptoms of a headache because it is much easier to get rid of it at that point. Once a headache reaches the migraine stage, it becomes very difficult to relax and get fast, complete results.

I want you to imagine now that you are looking at a pale blue screen. On the screen is the number 20. See the number 20 on the screen. Now let the 20 disappear, and go deeper. See the number 19, and let it disappear, and go deeper still. See 18, let it disappear ...17, and let it disappear...16, and let it disappear. A dark blue haze is forming on the screen...15...14... 13...deeper and darker blue...12... 11...10...the screen has now become a deep blue. Take a deep breath now and relax even more and watch your screen turn to purple with a gleaming number 10 on it. Now let the 10 dissolve into the purple, and see number 9 there. Now 8...7... 6...your screen is turning green now...5...4...3... 2...1...0. Now forget the numbers, forget the screen, and allow yourself to relax even more deeply.

Imagine yourself as you want to be...beautiful, free, and relaxed. Feeling good...looking wonderful ...feeling fine...full of health...full of strength, vitality, and joy...free of all pain...free of tension. This is you.

This is the real you. Every day from now on you will be more and more completely the woman you really want to be. You are just as capable, just as intelligent as anyone, even more so. Whatever needs to be done, you can do it because you are in control. From now on your control will be deeper and stronger all the time because you are relaxed and calm. Because you are relaxed and calm, your head will stay completely relaxed, your neck, spine, all over your body, you will be relaxed and free, and you will not have any more headaches at all. Never again will you have any headaches at all.

You will continue to do your self-hypnosis every day. If you begin to feel the first sign of a headache, you will do your self-hypnosis immediately, and each time you do the little self-hypnosis routine you will relax completely. You will go just as deep as you are now...just as deep as you are now or even deeper. Whatever suggestions you give yourself will go deeper and be stronger every time. Before you go to sleep at night you will do your self-hypnosis routine and give yourself the following suggestion: I will be relaxed and calm. I will sleep beautifully all night long and when I awaken I will feel just wonderful, and this will prevent a headache from starting at night.

Smoking

I want you to imagine now that you have a cigarette in your hand. See the smoke curling up and getting in your nose...it smells terrible, like burning garbage. See the smoke curling up from the tobacco and feel it getting into your eyes. It stings your nose and it burns and hurts your eyes. It smells rancid and dirty. It smells just awful...filthy and dirty. Now put the tobacco away; you put it down in the ashtray and you walk away...away from that dirty, awful, evil smelling smoke...glad to be free of that dirty tobacco. From now on you will be completely free of any desire for even a single puff of tobacco in any form. Whenever you think of smoking you will remember that dirty, awful smell and that foul taste, and you will be completely free of the desire for even a single puff of tobacco from now on.

I want you to imagine yourself. See yourself as you want to be. The real you...alive, healthy, full of vitality, full of strength, free from your former enslavement to that dirty tobacco. In control of your own behavior, feeling good, able to breathe again, able to smell things again and taste things again. This is you. This is the woman you can and will be. This is the woman you are now becoming. At this very moment you are making a promise to your self, not a promise to me, a promise to yourself...a commitment...a commitment that will grow stronger every day...a commitment to become the real you and stay completely away from tobacco from now on.

You will remain relaxed and calm. You will feel supremely confident that anything you set your mind to do, you can and will do. You will be successful and you will enjoy being successful. You will find it very easy to stay completely away from tobacco from now on. Because you will be relaxed and your mouth will be relaxed, you have no need or desire to smoke even a single puff ever again.

Every night you will sleep like a log, and the first thing you know it will be morning and you will awaken feeling on top of the world. The longer you stay away from tobacco, the easier it will be and the better you will feel every day. Whenever you practice your self-hypnosis exercise you will relax completely and very deeply. You will go just as deep as you are now. By practicing your self-hypnosis faithfully every day you will have absolute control over your desire to smoke. You will have the strength to stay away from, and you will stay away from, even the slightest inclination for a single puff.

This procedure refers to tobacco as smelling terrible, like burning garbage, and tasting filthy and dirty. In your actual use, substitute more effective words if you are able. The case example for diet control in chapter 3 used the specific taste and smell of wet chicken feathers to create a distaste for excessive popcorn consumption. If you are able, find specific smells and tastes that are repulsive to the subject and incorporate them into the smoking routine.

Chapter 13

Self-Hypnosis

It may seem redundant to include a separate chapter about self-hypnosis when this entire book is really about self-hypnosis, but there are some things that need to be explained that are not specifically covered elsewhere. The first twelve chapters provide the basic knowledge of this powerful tool called self-hypnosis. This chapter explores this topic in some depth.

The only significant difference between hypnosis and self-hypnosis is that in hypnosis the operator is one person and the subject is another person. In self-hypnosis, the operator and the subject are the same person.

If you have someone with whom you can share the learning experience of hypnosis, that is great. You can practice with each other, using the methods discussed in this book. This shared learning experience can be extremely valuable for both participants. It draws you closer together mentally and emotionally, and promotes mutual love and respect. It is also easier and faster to learn when you are working in partnership with someone.

Ask your partner to hypnotize you using a procedure similar to the one in session 2 (see chapter 3).

Then practice the self-hypnosis exercise for a few days. Have your partner again hypnotize you and reinforce the self-hypnosis suggestions. Again practice. The number of times you need reinforcement depends entirely on you. If you practice your self-hypnosis routine faithfully every day, one or two reinforcements may be sufficient. If your partner can take you through an entire six-session program as detailed in Part I, so much the better.

But what about the people who do not have someone to share the hypnosis learning experience? What can they do? How can they learn?

Put aside your concerns. This chapter brings into sharp focus everything discussed so far, adds a few modifications, and shows you how to do it easily, effectively, and inexpensively in the quiet solitude of whatever place you choose—all by yourself.

In chapter 11, the Cut Chin Case showed how I used self-hypnosis for pain control and healing. Other examples throughout the book convey the idea that self-hypnosis may be limitless in its potential for enriching one's life at every level of life.

You can indeed use self-hypnosis to solve virtually any problem. You can also use it to expand your awareness and tap into your innate higher intelligence and creative ability. When you use self-hypnosis for this second purpose, hypnosis becomes meditation. Self-hypnosis can also be used in those moments when you feel the need for the intervention of a higher power into some situation; it then becomes a form of prayer. The subtle differences in these uses of self-hypnosis lies in how you direct your thoughts

once you have altered your state of consciousness—
that is, have reached the alpha state. You'll find some
expanded uses of self-hypnosis that embrace the
realm of psychic experience in chapter 14. For the
moment, we will concern ourselves with the practical,
everyday uses.

Here is some fun I had with self-hypnosis. I was
scheduled to have two teeth extracted at the dentist's
office. The night before, I conditioned myself to control
the flow of my blood. The next day I quickly hypnotized myself as soon as I was reclined in the dentist's
chair. When the dentist pulled the teeth, I shut off the
blood flow from the wound left by the extractions. The
dentist was perplexed. He kept saying to his nurse,
"He isn't bleeding? Why isn't he bleeding? I don't
understand this." I smiled mentally. I couldn't smile
physically because of all the tools, cotton, and other
things stuffed in my mouth. As an aside, I also visualized fast, complete healing. The wounds were completely healed and the swelling gone within
seventy-two hours; the dentist had predicted one to
three weeks.

Here is how one of my clients had fun with self-
hypnosis. He was part of a group being studied at a
local hospital. The doctors were studying dreams.
Once a week, my client slept overnight in the hospital
with an electroencephalograph (EEG) attached to his
head. The EEG recorded his brain wave activity. By
watching it, the doctors could tell whether the brain
was in alpha, beta, theta, or delta and could also tell
when the sleeper was dreaming and when he was not.
My client immediately hypnotized himself as soon as

the machine was attached. The machine recorded deep alpha, indicative of sleep or dreaming—yet the man was obviously awake. One of the doctors said, "What's going on here?" Then the man alternately returned to beta, then alpha, then beta, then alpha and the machine faithfully recorded it. The changes drove the doctor crazy until the man finally told the doctor what he was doing. The doctor's reply isn't printable.

I have conceived and written nearly all of this book while in the alpha state. What does this mean? It means you can engage in activity and have your eyes open while still in an altered state of consciousness. Think about this a moment. What a powerful tool self-hypnosis is! It goes far beyond sitting quietly with closed eyes while directing your attention to a goal. To use self-hypnosis in this manner is not easily achievable. It requires a great deal of pre-conditioning while under hypnosis or self-hypnosis. This pre-conditioning would be similar to that for diet control, but with completely different suggestions; you will have to devise your own techniques and suggestions for this. Then it requires practice, practice, practice. Take my word for it, the time and effort are well worth the result. Develop your self-discipline and hang in there; you will succeed!

Now, are you hyped up enough to start? Then let us get down to the nitty-gritty.

Getting Started

To begin, you need some method of programming yourself with directions and suggestions. The first thing that probably comes to mind is to purchase pre-recorded hypnosis tapes already on the market and listen to them. Well, yes, that is one solution that will work; I do not have any quarrel with these commercially available hypnosis tapes, since I have several on the market. However, they can be expensive, and are often not tailored to your specific needs and desires; they are necessarily general in nature. For less money than commercial hypnosis tapes, purchase your own cassette tape recorder and a supply of blank tapes. Then make your own "tailored" tapes for your own situation.

Making your own tapes is my first recommendation. If you do not already have a cassette recorder, purchase an inexpensive one. You are only going to use it for voice, not high fidelity, so don't spend a lot of money. I have seen adequate cassette recorders in discount stores for $15 to $20; there is no need to spend more than $30. Purchase inexpensive blank tapes; again, this isn't for high fidelity, so you can be practical.

At this point, your next step depends on your specific desires with self-hypnosis.

Pre-Hypnosis Consultation

Yes, you should consult with yourself before learning to practice self-hypnosis.

This need not be an elaborate procedure, but it is an important one. Use some paper and a pen and write down the answers to these questions:

- Why do I want to learn self-hypnosis?
- What needs can I fill?
- What benefits can I gain?
- How can I help others also?
- What are my goals for self-hypnosis use?
- Am I dedicated enough to devote 15 minutes a day for the rest of my life to practice this valuable skill?

If you find it difficult or impossible to answer these questions, you probably are not ready for self-hypnosis. If this is the case, let the idea rest for a while. You can continue anytime when you become ready. Usually, if you try to pursue self-hypnosis before you are mentally and spiritually ready, it won't work well for you. Thus, you become discouraged and abandon the idea. If you have any doubts, wait awhile and pursue self-hypnosis when you are ready.

PRE-HYPNOSIS EXERCISES

Before you begin to learn self-hypnosis, use the following simple conditioning exercises.

Exercise 1

Sit down comfortably and face straight ahead. Roll your eyes upward as far as you can. This is quite uncomfortable. Hold your eyes upward for as long as you can. When the strain is more than you wish to continue enduring, close your eyes and let your eyes return to normal. Sit there with your eyes closed for a minute or two, relaxing and allowing your mind to be as blank as you can.

The benefit is that you have actually forced yourself into a light level of the alpha state. When the eyes roll upward, alpha is triggered. Since alpha is necessary for hypnosis, this exercise begins to train you (and your mind) for entering alpha at will.

Exercise 2

Sit down comfortably and close your eyes. Visualize the letters of your name slowly, one letter at a time. Then visualize your entire name all at once. Then erase your name and open your eyes.

This helps you develop your ability to visualize. Visualization is key to successful self-hypnosis and going beyond hypnosis into the psychic realm as described in chapter 15.

For many, visualization is difficult. Don't be discouraged if you have difficulty. If the first letter of your name is H and you are not able to visualize it, then mentally describe it to yourself...two vertical bars with a horizontal bar between them at midpoint...like a football goal post. Know in your intellect that the H is there. With practice, you will learn to visualize. As with any worthwhile skill, practice, practice, practice, and more practice makes perfect. This is as true for self-hypnosis as it is for playing a musical instrument. In hypnosis, you are learning to play the instrument of your mind. Whether you remain an amateur or advance to expert or something in between is entirely up to you and how much devotion, time, and integrity you are willing to invest.

SELF-HYPNOSIS ROUTINES

Case 1

Suppose your only desire is to solve a specific problem (for example, diet control) and not primarily to master self-hypnosis. Then record the diet control sessions found in Part I onto a cassette tape at a pace that is comfortable to you.

After you have recorded session 1, make yourself comfortable and play back the recording while letting yourself (via the recording) hypnotize you.

The next day, record session 2 and hypnotize yourself with it. The next day, session 3; the next day 4, and so on until session 6. After listening to all six sessions, you will have successfully achieved your goal of dealing constructively with the problem and learning a simple self-hypnosis routine in the process.

You do not have to do these six sessions in six consecutive days. You can space them up to a week apart and they will still be effective. When the spacing becomes greater than one week between sessions, the residual post-hypnotic suggestions tend to become weak or even ineffective.

For this six-session approach to solving a problem, do not do more than one session a day. The mind needs time to absorb and act upon one session before imposing another session on it.

If your problem is something other than diet, use the same method just described but tailor it toward your specific problem. There are enough suggestions and examples in this book for you to devise your own modifications. If smoking is the problem, you would say, "I will have no desire for cigarettes," instead of "I have no desire for chocolates."

Case 2

Suppose you do not want to deal with a specific problem at the moment. You just want to master self-hypnosis as a skill so you can later deal with any problem or situation when the need arises.

For this case, you will use your cassette recorder to hypnotize yourself for the initial training period. The following six steps are what I recommend you record to get started.

1. On the first day, record and listen to the entire session 1 (see chapter 2). Record these suggestions to session 1 at the proper time:

You are now beginning to learn how to hypnotize yourself for any worthwhile purpose you desire.

Every time you hear your voice on tape, you will respond to the directions and suggestions you give more effectively every time.

Every time you practice self-hypnosis, you will be able to do it faster and easier.

Soon you will be able to practice self-hypnosis very effectively without the aid of a recorder, and this is so.

2. On the second day, record and listen to routines A, B, C, D, E, F, G, and H in that order. Record the following after routine H:

You have now learned how to relax your mind and body. In the future, all you need to do to relax your mind and body this much or even more is to close your eyes and mentally count down from 10 to 1, or 5 to 1, or 3 to 1, visualizing each number as you think it.

You are learning the skills of self-hypnosis which you can practice anytime, any place, for any worthwhile purpose you choose.

3. On the third day, record and listen to routines A, B, I, and U in that order. Record the following after routine U:

This room is a very powerful place for you to come to practice your self-hypnosis. You can do anything you wish here. You create your own reality. You can bring anyone into your room you wish simply by asking them in. You can consult or converse with anyone here. The resources of universal intelligence are available to you here. You can solve problems, ask questions, practice any skill or speech, shed bad habits, adopt good habits, plan, program goals, seek inspiration and ideas, consult with your creator via prayer. There is no limit. No limit to what you can achieve in your room. It is your private inner space in your mind. It is your magic kingdom. It is your special domain from which you can control your life.

I am now going to stop speaking. Stay in your room for as long as you wish. When you are ready to leave your room, you may count slowly from one to five and open your eyes at the count of five.

NOTE: At this point you should not have anything

else on the tape to distract you. Just let the blank tape run; it will automatically shut off at the end. You remain in your room for as long as you wish, doing whatever programming and suggestions you wish, and counting yourself out from one to five when you are finished.

4. On the fourth day, record and listen to the following:

Sit comfortably in your chair and face straight ahead. Roll your eyes upward and focus your attention on a spot or object in your line of vision that is up high enough to make your eyes uncomfortable. About a forty-five degree upward angle of your eye movement.

Keep your eyes opened and focused on the spot. Take a deep breath and as you exhale mentally say the number 5 three times.

Now close your eyes and relax.

Take another deep breath, and as you exhale, mentally visualize and say the number 4 three times.

Take another breath, and as you exhale, mentally visualize and say the number 3 three times.

Again take a deep breath and as you exhale, mentally visualize and say the number 2 three times.

Once more, a deep breath and visualize and say the number 1 three times.

You are now deeply relaxed and you will continue to relax deeper and deeper with each breath you exhale.

As you continue to relax more and more completely, mentally repeat the following suggestions as I say them:

"I have now mastered the skill of self-hypnosis."

"I can use self-hypnosis anytime I wish, any place I wish for any worthwhile purpose I desire, and this is so."

"In the future, all I need to do to achieve levels of hypnosis this deep or even deeper is to close my eyes, take a deep breath, and slowly count 3...2...1 as I exhale. At that point, I can program my mind for any purpose I desire. I can go to my private room by simply visualizing my staircase, walking down my stairs, opening my door and entering my room where I can program for any purpose I desire."

5. On the fifth day, record and listen to the following:

Close your eyes, take a deep breath and as you exhale, mentally count three and visualize the 3, two and visualize the 2, one and visualize the 1.

Take a deep breath and continue to relax.

Now visualize your staircase. Go down your staircase and enter your room.

(Do not speak on the tape for ten seconds to allow yourself time to go to your room.)

You are in your room now. From now on you can enter self-hypnosis simply by closing your eyes, taking a deep breath, and mentally counting down from 3 to 1 while visualizing the numbers as you say them. At that point, you can do whatever programming or suggestions you wish.

For especially powerful programming and experiences, you can go to your room simply by visualizing your staircase and mentally descending the stairs to your room.

From now on you can awaken whenever you wish simply by desiring to do so and opening your eyes.

You no longer need the tape recording to enter or exit self-hypnosis. You can do it all by yourself whenever you wish. You may use the tape anytime you wish for refresher or for a special programming session that would be easier to do by tape if you choose, but you no longer are dependent on the use of the tape.

I am going to stop talking now. You may open your eyes and awaken whenever you wish.

6. On the sixth day and every day thereafter you do not need a recorder. You can simply close your eyes and do the 3...2...1 countdown. Then visualize your staircase, descend it, and enter your room. Stay in the room as long as you wish to do your programming and suggestions. Open your eyes when you wish to terminate the session. If you feel you want to awaken more slowly, count yourself out from 1 to 5, opening your eyes at the count of 5. I use the 1 to 5 count out most of the time because I really go quite deeply into alpha and theta.

NOTE: In these self-hypnosis sessions, it is all right to do more than one a day if you wish. Just don't let more than a week lapse between sessions; if you do, I recommend that you start over from the beginning for best results. Also, you may want to refresh yourself by listening to your tapes every once in awhile even though you have progressed beyond the point where you have to listen to them. Listening to them is kind of like putting a recharge on your battery. You may even want to create new tapes for special purposes.

Case 3

Suppose you don't have, can't afford, or don't want a cassette recorder. You can still achieve the same results, but it will require much more time and diligence.

If this is the case, do all the things exactly as outlined for Case 2 but without using a cassette recorder. This means you memorize everything and mentally instruct yourself while relaxing and listening to your mental commands.

Memorizing the commands is not simple to do. The part of your mind that gives the memorized instructions tends to want to go to beta level to do so. The part of your mind that wants to respond to the instructions and enter self-hypnosis must go to alpha level to do so.

As a result, your brain frequency tends to vacillate between beta and alpha. This simply means that each session is likely to be less effective than if you had a cassette recorder. Hence, you usually have to repeat these sessions a number of times to achieve results. But it still works well; just persevere and stick with it.

USES OF SELF-HYPNOSIS

Your subconscious mind is like an obedient servant; it will do whatever it is told. The subconscious does not reason; it just does. If you do not give directions to your subconscious mind, your mind will obey the directions you allow someone else to give it. If you do not establish a good self-image in your mind, and if you allow others to impress upon your mind that you are not a worthwhile person, then you will become a not very worthwhile person. Why is a child labeled "bad"? Perhaps parents, teachers, peers, and others verbally chastised him or her by saying, "You are a bad child!" when the child expressed themselves in an unacceptable manner. The child came to believe what the adults said. Although an act may be unacceptable, that doesn't make the child an unacceptable human being, but the child doesn't know that, so his or her mind becomes programmed "You are an unacceptable person" and a great deal of human damage has been done.

Fortunately, hypnosis can rectify the human damage.

If you have a poor self-image, use your self-hypnosis to change it to what you want.

If you have a habit you wish to rid yourself of—such as smoking, stuttering, or lying—get rid of it with self-hypnosis.

Improve your skills. If you need to speak in front of an audience, give the speech in your room under self-hypnosis the day before you have to deliver it. You will perfect the speech and perform it just the way you programmed yourself to perform.

Solve problems. Get information and advice from cosmic intelligence by asking for it. If Mahatma Gandhi is your hero, bring him into your room and ask him what you should do. Sound like science fiction? It isn't (see chapter 15).

Get rid of pain. Promote healing. Maintain your health. Live longer and better.

Establish contact with your own higher self—your spiritual self—your all-knowing self.

Set your goals and then enjoy life as your mind brings them into reality.

When I was a child I knew I wanted two things when I grew up. I wanted to grow a mustache, and I wanted to be a professional writer. I maintained those dreams, those images, faithfully. I didn't know it then, but I was engaging in *self-hypnosis.* I have had the mustache since I was nineteen years old (eons ago) and have been a professional writer since 1963. As an adult, I have other dreams and goals. Some have materialized (being a professional hypnotherapist, for example). Others are in process, and I can watch the events unfold with child-like excitement.

You, too, can make your dreams become reality by practicing self-hypnosis faithfully every day. You now know how to do it.

Chapter 14

Practical Applications

Up to this point, this book has provided the data you need to successfully use hypnosis and self-hypnosis for any worthwhile purpose you desire. You've read about an effective program for diet control and instructions on how to devise programs for things other than diet control. But even at this point many readers may be vague on exactly how to devise a program for their specific situation.

Although one book cannot cover the vast number of situations that exist, this chapter details instructions for a broad spectrum of situations. From this sampling, you will be able to do exactly what you want to do.

THE BUDDY SYSTEM

Some people prefer to work with others rather than alone. Once in awhile a person doesn't feel comfortable listening to her or his voice on tape. For people in these two categories, the buddy system is recommended.

(As far as listening to your own voice on tape is concerned, everyone finds it strange the first few

219

times, but you quickly adjust to it, and you will produce excellent results from your self-recorded hypnosis sessions.)

Two advantages of working by yourself are: You can work whenever you wish without having to coordinate your time with anyone, and you can work on highly personal situations.

Two advantages of working with a buddy are: You don't have to make tape recordings if you don't want to (your buddy reads the induction to you, and you read the induction procedure to your buddy; this gives you experience both as a hypnotist and as a subject), and two heads are often better than one in deciding what approach to use to handle a specific situation.

Whichever way you choose—alone or with a buddy —you can achieve excellent results. Most people ultimately use both approaches.

In choosing a buddy, pick someone who is seriously interested in hypnosis and self-improvement, just as you are. Pick someone who is sensitive and caring and who is not a blabbermouth who can't wait to spread it all over town that you are using self-hypnosis at age thirty-five to control nocturnal ejaculations.

Your buddy can be a spouse, sibling, parent, friend, business associate—anyone whom you trust and with whom you have a good rapport.

Hypnosis Clubs

A hypnosis club is the ultimate buddy system. Here a group of people with common interests gather to use hypnosis on each other to help each other in some way. It is great fun, and you can learn so much, so fast.

Members of hypnosis clubs can help each other gain self-esteem, love, confidence, freedom from pain, more energy and enthusiasm, better mental and physical health, and control over stress and depression.

Members can also help each other relax and control stress and eliminate boredom and the daily blahs. They can help each other breathe life and action into their innate creative abilities, help deal with spouse and children more effectively, and have greater appreciation of self.

Students who join a hypnosis club can find help with improving memory, taking tests, developing self-confidence and self-discipline, improving academic and athletic skills, and dealing with frustration and confusion.

A hypnosis club can be formal or informal. A formal club can write up a charter, develop membership requirements, charge dues to purchase tapes and books, and establish meeting times and places. An informal club can include members who agree to meet at a specific day and time. Each brings their copy of *Hypnosis for Beginners* and alternately become hypnotist and subject as they solve problems. They may even develop new procedures and experiment.

The beautiful thing about a hypnosis club is that there is no way you can achieve bad results. Nearly always, members achieve what is desired. However, if the subject doesn't cooperate, or if the operator has not yet developed sufficient skill, there may be no results. Remember, hypnosis is a learning process that requires much practice, so don't get upset when everything doesn't work out perfectly. There is no way you can cause harm to other members if you follow the guidelines and cautions given in this book.

Hypnosis clubs and groups are superb methods of mutual self-improvement. Members gain by being helped and gain by helping others.

Don't overlook the great opportunity of having your own family engage in group hypnosis. It is a marvelous way to increase love and understanding.

One rule for any group—whether a formal club, informal gathering, or family group—is sticking to a schedule. Meet every day if you wish, but do not be willy-nilly about the meetings. Meeting about once a week works best; set aside the time and make it happen. Disciplining the mind to produce the miracles you want requires persistence. In no case should you meet less frequently than once every other week because the residual effects of hypnotic suggestion usually wear off in about two weeks.

Guard against scheduling a meeting and then canceling or postponing it. That can become a counterproductive habit which ultimately can give zero results. An occasional rescheduling will likely be necessary from time to time, and that is all right. Just don't develop the habit of rescheduling, because when you do you are signaling your mind loud and clear, "My goals aren't very important. Reschedule them," and that is just what your mind will do: reschedule your goals so you won't attain them.

Hypnosis is more—much more—than just a set of words in a relaxing procedure. It is a way of life, a way of enjoying life to the fullest, a technique for creating and realizing the reality you want for yourself now and in the future. It is a vehicle you can drive through life in. The vehicle will only go where you direct it.

HABIT CONTROL

Case 1

If you want to control a habit and learn self-hypnosis at the same time, follow the six sessions detailed for diet control in Part I except for two things. First, delete all references and suggestions dealing with diet. Second, add appropriate references and suggestions for dealing with the habit you want to control.

For example, if nail biting is your problem, in session 2 you would not visualize putting a piece of chocolate in your mouth. Instead you would put your fingernail in your mouth and it would taste horrible. Let common sense prevail and you will do just fine.

Case 2

If you already have learned your self-hypnosis procedure, then, first, alter your state of consciousness with your simple self-hypnosis procedure. Second, give yourself appropriate suggestions for the particular habit. For example, in nail biting you might say the following:

I like myself and I am proud of who I am.

Ugly, stubby, chewed nails are not compatible with who I am.

When I put my fingers to my mouth to chew, I will immediately remember that I want long, beautiful nails that help enhance my appearance, and I will not bite my nails.

For situations other than nail biting, refer to chapter 9 for help in devising the suggestions you want to use. Use your common sense and be creative; you can come up with excellent suggestions.

Case 3

If you have not learned the self-hypnosis routine and do not wish to learn it but still want to deal with your habit problem, do the following eight steps. (As an alternative to recording each step, you could have a buddy say the words for you.)

1. Record hypnosis routines A, B, C, D, E, F, I, G, U, and V in that order.
2. After routine V, record the suggestions you wish to give yourself (for examples, see the suggestion in case 2 above or chapter 9).
3. Then record: I will now stop talking for three minutes while you visualize your desired goal.
4. Let the recorder continue to run for three minutes without anything being recorded. The purpose here is to allow time to visualize yourself and the goal you desire before more instructions are given. In the case of nail biting, visualize long, healthy, attractive fingernails, etc. Make the visualization as expansive, complete, and detailed as you wish for the project you are handling. If you think you want more than three minutes for this process, let the recorder run for whatever time you wish. There

is no magic number of minutes to visualize; it is your choice. If you are using the buddy system, your buddy should say, *"I am now going to stop talking for three minutes while you visualize."* Then she or he would simply remain silent for the required time before proceeding with the remaining hypnosis instructions.

5. Record hypnosis routines W and 1J. In routine W, delete references to diet and substitute other appropriate words.

Your finished tape should have the following data on it: routines A, B, C, D, E, F, G, I, U, and V; your specific suggestions for self-help; a blank pause for X number of minutes to allow time for your visualization of success; and routines W and 1J.

6. Close your eyes and replay the recording, hypnotizing yourself. (This step is not necessary if your buddy did the hypnotizing in person.)

7. Listen to the tape once every day (more often if you wish) until the desired results are obtained. That is, until you get rid of your unwanted habit. If you are using the buddy system, your buddy would have to say the routines every day for you—a very clear advantage for making your own tape.

8. If the unwanted habit starts to recur, get out your tape and use it daily until the problem disappears. It is rare that you will have to do this more than once after your initial handling of the problem.

For the remaining uses described in this chapter, you'll find only the routines and suggestions as described in *Case 3* above under the assumption that you are interested in quickly dealing with the problem by yourself. In all situations, however, you may exercise your own self-hypnosis procedure (as in *Case 2* above) or a full-blown procedure where you learn self-hypnosis (as in *Case 1* above). You may use the buddy system also if you wish in any of the following situations.

Following are general approaches and specifics for each situation without a repetition of all the routine detail and the options and variations. Just become familiar with the options detailed here under *Habit Control*—those same options apply to all the other situations.

Phobias

Agoraphobia

The dictionary defines *agoraphobia* as "morbid fear of being in an open space." People with this phobia panic when in open places such as supermarkets, shopping centers, and parks. These people usually confine themselves to their home or automobile. In severe cases, people will not leave their home at all. Many will leave but only in their car. They will drive someone somewhere, but won't get out of the car themselves. Others will force themselves to make a quick run into a grocery store for a much needed item and get out as quickly as they can, all the time in terror of having a panic attack.

There is no need for these people to continue leading such unhappy lives. Hypnosis can help.

The following seven-step procedure will help.

1. Record hypnosis routines A, B, C, D, E, F, I, G, U, and V.
2. Record the following suggestions (or if you prefer, make up your own):

I am a worthwhile person, and I am thankful to be alive.

My Creator gave me the entire world to enjoy and to use for my benefit. This includes small cramped spaces and it includes large wide open spaces.

I am now making a commitment to myself to enjoy all of creation, especially all open spaces, large areas, crowds, everything.

There is no need to fear being in an open or large place because my Creator gave it to me with love to enjoy and use. He never gives me anything that I should ever fear, and this is so.

I love all of my world, and I intend to use all of it, and enjoy it, and learn from it.

I give thanks to my Creator for everything He has given me.

3. Then record the following:

I want you to imagine now that you are strolling through a large public park. You are walking alone, but there are other people whom you can see walking in the park. It is a warm, sunny day and you have a smile on your face. You feel great and at peace with the entire world. This is a spacious place. You seem to be able to see forever in all directions. You love it here. You can hear the birds singing in the lush treetops.

Occasionally you meet someone on the path you are walking and they smile and say, "Have a nice day." You smile back and wish them well. What a beautiful place. What a beautiful world. It is not confining you. You can do whatever you want and go in whatever direction you wish. Perfect freedom. You love the spaciousness and enjoy the peace and the experience of being here and of learning all you can about events that take place here. You come to a broad city street and across the street is a large shopping center. It is a huge, roomy place with crowds of shoppers scurrying about. What a delightful place to be. Enter the first shop you come to and browse through all the merchandise there. Pick out some things you like and purchase them. What fun. You love mingling with the people who are having fun just like you. Your smile is so strong that it just may stay on your face permanently. What a beautiful world you live in. Now take your purchases and walk back across the street and into the park again. This has been a perfect outing and you vow to get out more often into the wide open spaces where you can benefit from more of your marvelous world.

NOTE: Devise your own visualization procedure in place of this one if you prefer. Keep the same concept of enjoying the wide open spaces that your Creator gave you for your benefit.

4. Record routines W and 1J, deleting any diet references.

    Your finished tape should have the following data on it: routines A, B, C, D, E, F, I, G, U, and V; your specific suggestions for self-help; your visualization instructions; and routines W and 1J.

5. Close your eyes and replay your tape, hypnotizing yourself.
6. Listen to your tape every day at least once until you no longer have the problem.
7. If the problem starts to recur, listen to your tape again until the problem disappears.

Claustrophobia

The dictionary defines *claustrophobia* as "morbid dread of closed or narrow places." People with this phobia panic when in small, closed, or narrow places. They avoid going into closets. Putting something over their head would send them into panic. Sometimes even a large passenger car is too confining for them.

As with all phobias, hypnosis can help people who are claustrophobic.

Follow the same procedure as detailed in the Agoraphobia section above. Following are some suggestions to use in step 2.

I am a worthwhile person, and I am thankful to be alive.

My Creator gave me the entire world to enjoy and use for my benefit. This includes small cramped spaces as well as large, open spaces.

I am now making a commitment to myself to enjoy all of creation, especially all small, narrow, or cramped spaces, everything.

There is no need to fear being in small, closed, or tight places because my Creator gave it to me with love to enjoy and use. He never gives me anything that I should ever fear, and this is so.

I love all of my world, and I intend to use all of it, and enjoy it, and learn from it.

I give thanks to my Creator for everything He has given me.

Following are visualization instructions for step 3.

I want you to imagine now that you have just walked into a closet where you store books, magazines, and photographs. The closet has a light in it and you turn it on. This is a tiny closet packed with your private literature. You have come in here to get your favorite book to read so you can spend a quiet, peaceful day reading. A draft blows the closet door shut, locking you inside. At that moment, the phone rings in the living room. You listen to the phone ring and you smile because now you don't have to answer it and have your quiet day interrupted. There is just enough space on the floor to sit comfortably and read. The idea of being locked in really tickles your fancy because now you have a legitimate excuse for not doing anything except enjoy yourself reading, relaxing, browsing through old photographs, and reminiscing. A perfect, quiet, peaceful afternoon with no intrusions from anyone or anything. You love it. You know the key to the door is in your pocket, but you are going to ignore that. Instead you are pretending to be locked in so you can enjoy the solitude of your own private space. Being cramped appeals to you because it brings your friends, the books and photos, close to you where you can feel the warmth of their presence. What a lovely, calm, peaceful way to spend the day. You vow to retreat into your own tiny space in the closet every once

*in awhile so you can enjoy just being with yourself.
You hadn't realized before just how cozy and secure
this experience could be. You love it.*

NOTE: Devise your own visualization procedure in
place of this one if you prefer. Keep the same concept
of enjoying the tiny, cramped space that your Creator
gave you for your benefit.

Other Phobias

Follow the same pattern as for the two phobias
described above. All you need to change are the specific suggestions you give yourself and the visualization instructions you create.

Make your suggestions and visualizations in the
same positive vein: give thanks for what you have and
who you are; show appreciation for yourself; enjoy all
situations that have caused you problems in the past.
Let your creative mind run free in devising vivid, powerful visualizations and suggestions. There is no limit
to what you can achieve if you diligently put your
mind to it.

SENIOR CITIZENS

Many senior citizens are beset with a myriad of problems. They have been released from the job market,
and they often feel useless. The aging process often
leaves them with aches, pains, and physical debilities
that frustrate them because it stops them from enjoying more of life. Their income is limited, often to
poverty levels. They want to do constructive work, but

have difficulty finding anything. Their families are grown and have their own problems, leaving the senior citizen to feel abandoned. They crave companionship, but don't know how to find it. Their self-esteem slips, and they become depressed.

While there are many senior citizens who do not have the above problems, many do. There is no reason why anyone of any age should not enjoy life to the fullest. Hypnosis can help.

Follow the same seven-step procedure used in the preceding situations in this chapter.

1. Record hypnosis routines A, B, C, D, E, F, I, G, U, and V.
2. Record specific suggestions for the situations you are dealing with. Some suggestions you might consider using:

I am a worthwhile person, and I am thankful to be alive.

I am happy to be the age I am because I have earned the right by my past daily living and experiences.

I am delighted to be my present age because I am much wiser and more experienced than I used to be.

I have many beautiful memories to comfort me at all times.

There are many worthwhile things that I can do, and I am learning to do more by using my mind to create my reality as I want it to be.

I command my creative mind to furnish me with ideas and thoughts that will enable me to enrich my life more and more.

I command my mind to furnish me with the physical fortitude to live each day with ever increasing achievement and enjoyment.

I thank my Creator for my life and my state of life.

I ask for the insight to use my innate abilities for greater benefit to myself and others.

I give thanks to my Creator for everything He has given me.

I enjoy being with other people, but I also enjoy being alone.

I am in control of my own life, and I accept responsibility for taking care of myself to the fullest extent of my ability.

3. Record visualization instructions that you create to deal with the specific situation you have in mind. One visualization technique you may want to use is the Seashore Trip in chapter 12. This is an especially powerful routine. While you are on the beach, visualize yourself successfully doing anything you enjoy.

4. Record hypnosis routines W and 1J, deleting any references to diet.

5. Relax and play back your tape recording, hypnotizing yourself.

6. Listen to your tape every day at least once, until you no longer have the problem.

7. If the problem starts to recur, listen to your tape again until the problem disappears.

I am now a senior citizen, and I had the experience of being cut from the job market prematurely.

Fortunately, my wife and I had the foresight and financial management skills so that we were not left in a critical situation. However, I still needed to work because at the time neither of us was close to being eligible for social security. (Yet I was old enough that the marketplace wasn't interested in hiring me; an all too common situation for many people.) If I didn't find work within a reasonable time, we would have a critical situation. What did I do to find work? First, I took stock of what I could do that had no relationship to age. Here is what I came up with:

I am a very good writer.

I am an excellent hypnotist.

I am a good astrologer.

I am a good lecturer and teacher.

I love doing all the above things.

Using my self-hypnosis, I set my goals and brought them into reality. My results:

Until I reached retirement age, I earned a very nice living doing contract technical writing for various industries.

I wrote a number of books on astrology, hypnosis, self-improvement, and psychic development, and they were all successfully published.

I have written and sold many magazine articles.

I gave lectures on altered states of consciousness, psychic development, and hypnosis.

I purchased five timeshare villas in Cancun, Mexico; we have a lovely place to vacation several times a year for the rest of our lives.

I enjoy good health because I programmed it that way with self-hypnosis.

My wife and I are now retired, and I continue to write and lecture, but on a less demanding schedule.

I have a full life of freedom, enjoyment, and achievement. And it is all because of how I use my altered state of consciousness via self-hypnosis and psychic practice (the next step beyond hypnosis).

You can do the same or even more. You have at least one ability that you can capitalize on, and most likely much more than that. Start using your head, your altered state of consciousness, and your creative mind, and make good things happen for yourself. Don't depend on others. Rely on yourself. You can do it. This book gives you the key, but you must use the key to unlock your own doors to your own rewarding future.

Families of Senior Citizens

Often, family members of a senior citizen feel their lifestyle is cramped. Or they feel guilty about not doing more for the senior member. Or they feel the person is a bother. There are many reasons why family members feel stress. Self-hypnosis can help handle all of these reasons.

Use the same general program detailed previously in this chapter.

The hypnosis induction procedures in themselves do a great deal to release tension and stress. In step 2, include good, loving suggestions for yourself and for the senior person in your family:

I am a worthwhile person, and I am thankful to be alive.

(Name of the elderly person) *is a worthwhile person, and I am thankful to be associated with her or him, and I love her or him.*

I will show my love and appreciation for (name of person) *every day by listening to her or him more attentively and treating her or him with more respect and gentleness.*

I will allow (name of person) *to be independent and will not try to impose my ideas and desires on her or him.*

I will encourage (name of person) *to engage in whatever activity she or he wants that brings she or he enjoyment and benefit.*

For the visualization in step 3, use the Seashore Trip in chapter 12. While on the beach, visualize yourself happily engaging in conversation or beneficial activity with the senior citizen.

Remember, senior citizens have a great deal of wisdom and experience to share if you allow it. You benefit from their counsel, and they gain self-esteem from giving it.

SHUT-INS

Shut-ins are people who are completely or predominantly confined to a home or institution. Among these are people who are bedridden, people in wheelchairs or otherwise restricted in their movement, prisoners, those temporarily confined due to bad weather; and those who are unemployed with a great deal of time on their hands.

These people are offered a great opportunity: time.

Time can work for or against you as you choose. This book shows you how to make time work for you. Anyone can improve their circumstances if they choose to do so. Everyone classified as a shut-in has an abundance of time to devote to self-improvement—start doing so immediately. Because time is on your side, you have a big advantage over those who have a limited amount of time to devote to self-improvement.

Learn your self-hypnosis technique. Practice many times every day. Become an expert. You can do it in record time because you have time.

Here are a few suggestions toward correcting whatever physical problems you have, improving your self-image, improving your mental attitude, and discovering and using your hidden talents (for example, in bed you can write, paint, operate a telephone answering service, or do telephone soliciting).

Some suggestions to give yourself in step 2:

I am a worthwhile person, and I am thankful to be alive.

I am making a commitment to myself to discover and use all the faculties I can muster.

I direct all my innate healing energies to my (name of the part of your body that is ailing), and I am healing one hundred times faster than normal.

I enjoy life, and I am learning to enjoy life more and more each day.

I am triumphing over all obstacles, and this is so.

I send love to all who have been kind to me.

I forgive all who have been unkind to me and send

them love also.

I forgive myself for all past transgressions.

Some ideas for the visualization in step 3 are:

Use the Seashore Trip routine (chapter 12) to send love and forgiveness and to create a happy, fulfilling future for yourself.

Visualize yourself actively engaged in successfully performing some work or hobby that you enjoy.

Visualize yourself happy, energetic, and healthy.

Disabled

Read the preceding section because all of that can be applied to you. In addition, you have additional capabilities because you are probably able to be somewhat mobile. This means an even greater possibility for jobs and hobbies. Exercise your imagination. Use your self-hypnosis to gain the awareness you need to expand your horizons. It really works.

An additional suggestion for step 2:

I am rapidly overcoming my temporary disability and learning to live a more fulfilling and rewarding life.

NOTE: Use the word "temporary." Even if your physician or someone else says your condition is permanent, do not accept it as your reality. They have made their best judgment, but you have the right to exercise your best judgment too. After all, it is your life. Use your hypnosis to enjoy life within the constraints of your current condition, but never give in to your current condition. Always strive for improvement. If you do not realize improvement for whatever reason, that is all right—as long as you diligently strive for the improvement, because in so doing, you enrich your life in some measure. The only people who fail are those who give up. Devise your own additional suggestions.

An additional visualization idea for step 3:

Create your ideal work situation in great detail. See yourself successfully performing. See yourself successfully interacting with others. See yourself doing everything perfectly. Then tell yourself: This is my new reality, and I command my higher mind to manifest it into the physical world.

Prisoners

Make your time work for you by becoming an expert at self-hypnosis and creating a new, enjoyable life for yourself. To do so requires perseverance and time; make it happen. There are many things you need to address, including guilt and forgiveness, attitude, self-esteem, enthusiasm, faith in self, self-control, responsibility, and rights of self and rights of others.

A few suggestions for step 2:

I accept responsibility for who I am and for everything I have done and will do in the future.

I am making a commitment to myself to conduct myself in a responsible manner as a citizen of the Universe.

I am a worthwhile person, and I am thankful to be alive.

I intend to use the rest of my life in a peaceful, enjoyable way.

I vow to myself to act with honor, success, distinction, and integrity in all present and future endeavors.

I forgive myself for all errors in judgment and behavior and I am determined to do better.

I forgive all others without reservation for their errors in judgment and behavior.

I command my higher self to bring me the awareness and ability to create a better life for myself and for others.

Some visualization ideas for step 3:

Use the Seashore Trip (chapter 12) to send forgiveness and love. Also use it to close the door to the past and open the door to the future. When you are on the beach facing the sea of life, the door to the past is on your right, and the door to the future is on your left. Go to the door of the past, shut it, lock it, and throw the key into the sea where it cannot be recovered. Then go to the door of the future, unlock it, open it wide, and put the key in your pocket (you hold the key to your future). Look through the door to the future and visualize yourself as you wish to be.

Visualize yourself shaking the warden's hand and walking away from the prison as a free person.

Visualize yourself interviewing successfully for a job and getting the job. See yourself performing competently on the job.

Even while you are still in prison, visualize yourself getting along well with the other prisoners and the prison officials. See yourself as a person who is respected by all.

If tapes and a cassette player are not available to you, you will have to memorize the procedures and say them back to yourself mentally. I realize this takes more time, but you have the time. Good luck!

Bad Weather Blahs

Being inside because of bad weather is a blessing in disguise. Instead of grumping about being captive at home because of what you perceive as foul weather, be glad for it. First, the truth is that all sorts of weather are needed whether you see the need or not. Second, the weather gives you an excellent excuse to use the time to your benefit by enriching your life through self-hypnosis.

Some suggestions for step 2:

I am a worthwhile person, and I am glad to be alive and to be exactly where I am at this moment.

I welcome the opportunity to improve my life through self-hypnosis.

Today's weather is needed for some good reason, and I am glad for it.

Engage in self-improvement by giving yourself suggestions for anything you have in mind, be it improving your Bridge game; improving your relationship with family members or neighbors; seeking a new job; or improving health.

Your visualizations in step 3 can be anything already discussed or something new. Let your mind run unfettered. But whatever you visualize, always see yourself happy and successful.

Unemployed

Use suggestions from the "Increasing Self-Confidence" and "Improving Work Success" sections of chapter 9.

Visualize yourself successfully interviewing for a job and getting it. See yourself happy and performing well on the job of your choice.

PAIN CONTROL

There are four kinds of pain: headaches; persistent chronic pain such as from arthritis or a nagging backache; sharp, usually shorter duration pain such as from a cut, burn, or stubbed toe; and pain caused by various illnesses that can range for short duration to long duration. Hypnosis can relieve or greatly reduce all of these.

For pain control, first learn your self-hypnosis procedure and practice it daily, even if only for a few minutes every day. That way, when you experience a pain, you can alter your state of consciousness within seconds and deal with the pain.

Here is what the scenario might be

If you did not know a self-hypnosis routine and had to rely solely on tape recorded procedures, the following scenario might take place:

1. You burn your finger on the stove while cooking. It really hurts.
2. You look for your cassette recorder.
3. You search for a blank tape.

4. You look for your copy of this book and find the induction procedure.
5. You record ten induction procedures, the suggestions for "no pain," the visualization instructions for perfect healing, and the closing hypnosis routines.
6. You rewind the tape, sit down, and play it back to hypnotize yourself.

It's a ludicrous scene—by the time you are ready to deal with the problem, thirty minutes have lapsed. In the meantime, your burn blistered and you had the pain or discomfort the entire time. Obviously, this is not the most intelligent way to handle this kind of emergency pain with hypnosis.

The intelligent way is to already know your self-hypnosis procedure by memory so you can deal with the problem within seconds, avoiding prolonged discomfort. Reread the Cut Chin Case in chapter 11 to see how to deal with this kind of situation.

If you have chronic pain, such as from arthritis or frequent migraines, prepare a tape in advance and have it ready to go when you need it.

The best way to handle all pain is to memorize the short self-hypnosis procedure so you can use it anytime, anywhere instantly.

Injury and Healing

The preceding section also applies to injuries and healing. But knowing self-hypnosis by memory also enables you to help someone else on the spur of the moment. You never know when an opportunity to help someone else will occur (such as helping the little girl with her ear ache described in chapter 11). Here is another spur-of-the-moment case where I was able to help a woman with a medical problem.

My wife, Dee, and I frequently go to estate sales. We see many of the same people over a period of time and develop a casual speaking acquaintance with them.

Estate sales are chaotic. Dozens of people run around, look at merchandise, talk, and fall all over each other. Workers move large pieces of furniture and yell for people to clear a way for them.

At one of these sales, my wife noticed one of our casual acquaintances sitting in a chair in the corner of one of the most chaotic rooms. The woman usually bustled with energy and smiled, but now she sat with an expression that said something was very wrong.

Dee walked over to her and asked, "Mary, are you all right?"

"No," she answered. "I'm having a severe vertigo attack and had to sit to keep from falling." She explained that she had suffered from vertigo for many years. At first medication had helped, but now it didn't help at all. In addition to causing her to lose her balance, her eyesight became blurred and she felt dizzy and somewhat nauseous.

"My husband is a hypnotherapist," my wife said. "Would you like him to help you right now?"

"I would appreciate anything he could do," Mary answered.

Dee called me over and explained the situation.

"Mary," I asked, "would you allow me to hypnotize you right now where you are sitting?" When she agreed, I stood close to her and leaned over so my mouth was only inches from her right ear. I wanted to speak to her in a normal tone of voice and have her be able to understand me over all the noise that surrounded us.

I told her to close her eyes. I did a ten to one countdown, a head to toe relaxation, and then the staircase routine (routine U).

While she was in her room in routine U, I filled her with white healing light. I intensified the light between her ears (vertigo is caused by inner ear problems) and told her that the light had cured her vertigo. Then I counted her out from one to five.

She smiled. "I feel wonderful," she said. The vertigo was gone. She got up and enjoyed the rest of the estate sale.

Several weeks later we saw her again, and she rushed over to tell me that she has not had an attack since the hypnosis. She said she usually had them at least several times a week and sometimes daily.

So memorize your hypnosis routines, at least a few of them, so you can help others. If you have a friend who is bedridden while recovering from surgery, ask if you can hypnotize her or him and give suggestions to ease the discomfort and promote the healing (reread the Cut Foot Case in chapter 11 for suggestions).

If you encounter an emergency situation such as an auto accident and medical help has not yet arrived, use hypnosis to make the injured more comfortable. In this case don't say, "I am going to hypnotize you." Instead, approach the victim and try to make him comfortable with a blanket or coat. Unless his life is in immediate danger, do not move him because you may cause damage. Talk confidently and calmly and say, "I will help you relax and feel better until medical help arrives. Just listen to my voice and follow my instructions." Then go through a few brief relaxation procedures and give the person suggestions for becoming more comfortable and having strength to persevere until medical help arrives. This type of situation calls for improvising and quick thinking. That is why it is important to become an expert in hypnosis in case you can be of help.

One note of caution: If you assist in a serious accident situation, do not do or say anything to give the victim cause for concern. For example, if the victim says, "I can't feel my right foot. Is it all right?" Do not say, "It is practically severed so you probably can't feel it because the nerves are cut." Instead say, "Don't be concerned about anything. You look all right to me. Let's wait for medical help on these matters. In the meantime, let's concentrate on feeling more relaxed and comfortable." One more thing: if the victim is bleeding, do what you can to stop the blood flow, all the while talking calmly to relax the person.

BUSINESS USES

There is probably no greater use for self-hypnosis than in business. The business world is plagued with stress, excessive alcohol abuse (probably because of the stress), health problems such as heart attacks (again probably due to stress), absenteeism, work attitude problems, and mediocre performance. Yet, ironically, business and industry seem to deliberately shun hypnosis as a viable tool.

I worked as a contract technical writer for three different companies that had the problems mentioned above. In each case I made a presentation to key managers and executives on how hypnosis could effectively reduce or alleviate many of their problems. Since they were already paying me to write, I suggested they allow me to give seminars to teach volunteers how to use self-hypnosis. I offered to deal on a one-to-one basis with problem cases. I would not charge any fee for these services. I would put in the needed extra time on my own.

In each case, I was laughed out of the office. One executive gave polite excuses while fighting to control his laughter. Another was quite nasty. The third just said a loud, defiant "No!"

How shortsighted these executives were. Unfortunately, their shortsightedness must have run into other aspects of their decision making—all three companies went bankrupt shortly after my contract with them expired.

If there is one manager, one executive, one person of influence in business reading this book, I implore you to consider the contents in relation to your business. Most of your key problems are people problems; hypnosis can deal effectively with them. The most successful way to fail is to not take a chance. So be bold and take a chance for the sake of your business and for the sake of all the fine people in your business.

This book gives you all you need to know. There is no need for me to detail additional specific suggestions.

Consulting With a Higher Authority

Perhaps the most valuable tool this book offers is the mechanism for consulting with higher authority for guidance and help. By higher authority I mean anyone, living or deceased, who represents higher authority to you, including your Creator, Jesus Christ, Buddha, Krishna, Confucius, Mohandas Gandhi, the prophet Mohammed, Moses, Abraham, a parent, friend, or business associate, a president, past or present—literally anyone.

For example, if you are an engineer and are wrestling with a difficult engineering problem, you might want to consult with the great inventor Nikola Tesla. If you are a writer and are having difficulty with the novel you are writing, you might want to consult with Harper Lee or some other fine author. A diplomat might want to consult with Benjamin Franklin. Just follow these four steps:

1. Record hypnosis routines A, B, C, D, E, F, G, U, and V.
2. Replay the tape and allow it to hypnotize you and take you to your own private inner room. (You will be in your room after routine V finishes.)
3. Stay in your room for as long as you wish. This is where you will do your consulting with higher authority. Don't be concerned about the tape running; it has nothing on it and will automatically shut off at the end of the reel.
4. While in your room, invite whomever you wish into your room. You can issue your request mentally or out loud.

Here is how I do it. After I am in my room, I mentally say, "I ask that my friend, consultant, and guide Mohandas Gandhi enter my room and help me. I need your wisdom and counsel at this time." Then I press a button I have in my room that opens a door through which my guest may enter.

When Gandhi enters, I talk to him just as I would anyone. I explain my problem or question and listen for advice. We communicate. When I have what I need, and if he has no further things to say, I thank him for coming. He leaves and the door closes.

I do all this silently in my mind, but you can do it aloud if you wish. I find the sound of my voice is sometimes distracting, so I most often speak mentally or in a whisper, and sense my guest's reply mentally.

This method works because your higher mind is in direct contact with the higher mind of your guest. For that reason, you could consult with a newborn baby and receive intelligent, valuable information. The baby's higher mind is part of cosmic intelligence even though the baby's conscious mind has not yet developed.

This whole experience is really a spiritual one and is powerful. Gandhi has given me a great deal of valuable help. So have some others I have invited into my room.

Each person has her or his own unique experience in inviting someone into their room and consulting. Some see the person enter and hear her or his voice (I usually do). Some sense the presence and the information, but do not actually see or hear it (I have had this experience also). Some do not see or sense anything, but they pretend the presence is there and carry on their conversation (I have done this many times). All of these situations are valid and work.

Sometimes you get the information you need right then and there in the room. Other times you seem to get nothing at the moment, but later when you least expect it, the information comes booming into your mind. Don't give up; it works, and it is exciting.

I have had the information I requested come to me while driving my car hours (or even a day or two later) after the session in my room. Always, you should receive the guidance you need within seventy-two hours after consulting with your guest. If not, repeat the consulting session. Persist until you get what you want. Each time it becomes easier and more effective.

Often the guidance you seek can come to you in subtle or strange ways. I buy a newspaper only on Wednesday and Sunday because those two issues contain all the ads, recap of the week's news, and the best comics. One Sunday evening I went to my room to consult with Ernest Hemingway. I wanted to quit my current employment and devote my life to writing, lecturing, and helping people through hypnosis. I was greatly reluctant to take the chance. I had been with my employer for eighteen years and was an executive with a comfortable salary. To quit for something as nebulous as I envisioned seemed foolhardy. I explained my situation to Hemingway. He said absolutely nothing; he just listened. I thanked him for coming, and he left.

The next morning while driving to work, I had an overpowering urge to purchase a newspaper. To me, the Monday morning paper is the most useless of all daily papers, and here I was buying it on impulse. I browsed through it later at lunch. Buried in one of the inside pages was a filler article. It read, "There are many excellent ways to achieve failure, but not taking a chance is the most successful." Those words leapt off the page and told me what I needed to know. I would take a chance and quit my job, and I would be successful at what I wanted to do. So I did, and I am.

I recommend you explore this great communication path with higher intelligence.

SLEEP

There is one more very powerful, easy-to-implement usage for hypnosis: going to sleep while listening to a hypnosis tape you have recorded. I'm not just talking about using it to help you sleep better—although you can use it for that also—I am talking about any purpose you desire.

Neither your subconscious mind nor your hearing faculties ever go to sleep. Therefore, even though you fall asleep while your tape is playing, your mind absorbs everything on the tape and begins the process of making your reality materialize. While asleep, you are in a deep hypnotic state, so the tape works wonders. Follow these three steps.

1. Record routines A, B, C, D, E, F, I, G, U, and V followed by specific suggestions you wish to have become reality.

2. When you lay down to go to sleep, turn on the recorder and drift off to sleep while it plays.
3. The recorder will automatically shut off at the end, not causing you to wake up.

In these bedtime tapes I do not include visualization instructions, only verbal suggestions. It works quite well. For example, suppose you have a job interview scheduled for the next day. Make the tape and put in appropriate suggestions for your success in giving a good interview. You will be calm, speak intelligently, be charming without being gushy, etc. (see chapter 9 for some good interview suggestions). Then go to sleep while your tape does the work. The next day you will have a fine interview.

CHAPTER 15

The Next Step

Everything you've read up to this point enables you to enrich your life in whatever manner you choose using hypnosis and self-hypnosis. This chapter provides information to launch yourself even further than the wonders of self-hypnosis into the awesome realm of psychic experience.

THE PSYCHIC REALM

Words such as *visualization, alpha,* and *theta* have appeared throughout this book. Many references have been made to something beyond hypnosis and you've been told that your abilities are nearly limitless. Strong hints have been made that there are things you can do in addition to the marvelous, exciting things already discussed. You've already learned how to tailor and reshape your entire life in every respect if you choose to. What more could there possibly be?

If your hypnosis learning experience were likened to our traditional school system, at this point I would say, "You have just graduated from kindergarten!" Reflect on that a moment. You have just learned one of the most powerful, useful, and exciting skills imaginable—and I say that brings you through kindergarten. You must conclude then that there must be an awesome amount to experience beyond what we call self-hypnosis.

Indeed, there is an awesome amount to experience. You have the ability to develop your sixth sense (your psychic sense) and use it just as readily as you use self-hypnosis. Hypnosis takes you to, and through, the door to the psychic realm in some of the exercises in this book. For example, going into your room in routine U and communicating with other intelligent beings is in the psychic realm.

The psychic realm embraces such things as mental telepathy, psychic healing, clairvoyance, psychometry, and much more. You already have a sixth sense (innate psychic ability) given to you as a birthright, but you haven't developed it and used it to its fullest extent. Hypnosis gives you an excellent start in entering into psychic development. Hypnosis training and experience are not required in order to develop your psychic ability, but you can develop your psychic ability much faster and go into deeper, more meaningful experiences if you first have hypnosis training and experience.

Ponder for a moment about where we live, who we are, and what life is all about. You experience life as a human being in just one dimension on a tiny planet in one incredibly vast universe out of many universes. How many dimensions are there? We don't know, but we know there are many. How many universes? Many. When you think about these things, it makes you feel very insignificant. Well, we are insignificant—physically.

We are really not physical beings. We are merely housed temporarily in a container that we call a body. We are intelligent beings—spiritual beings—living, eternal energies that always have been and always will be. We are a significant part of the total cosmic intelligence, and as such we have access to any of the information within that cosmic intelligence. Now you don't feel so insignificant any longer, do you?

Well, you should never feel insignificant because you are a participating member of all that is. Be humble, yes. Modest, yes. But never insignificant.

The implications of what I just said are enormous and mind boggling. Did I just imply that somehow you have access to information from other dimensions, from other worlds, from other minds? Yes, that is exactly my implication. It is more than just an implication—it is truth.

How?

You have already made a start with your self-hypnosis. If you care to go even further into the psychic realm, I recommend you read my book *Psychic Development for Beginners* (Llewellyn Publications, 1996).

Visualization

Visualization is the key to success in your self-hypnosis and to entering the domain of psychic experience. The more vividly you can visualize, create, and hold mental pictures, the greater your ability to connect with any intelligent experience. You can converse with Gandhi by going to your room, inviting him in, and visualizing him there. Gandhi's temporary house, his body, is dead, but he lives on as an intelligent energy in some dimension, and he is available to you. All intelligent energies are available to you without restriction.

You can go anywhere at a mental intelligence level without your physical body leaving the room. This is astral travel. Visualization helps achieve this.

Alpha

You can achieve every thing discussed in the first fourteen chapters by going to the alpha level—anywhere in the alpha level. The deeper you go into alpha (lower frequency), the closer you get to theta, and the more profound your experiences become. To go into the psychic realm, you need to function in the theta level for the most profound experiences. It is possible, however, to also have psychic experience in the alpha level.

Theta

At this level, you are able to experience astral travel, communication with other minds or intelligence sources, tap the resources of universal intelligence, and experience profound enlightenment.

Getting to theta is relatively easy. First, become very skilled at self-hypnosis so you have your mind trained to drop into alpha instantly by a mere wish to do so. This will happen for you automatically if you practice self-hypnosis at least fifteen minutes every day with integrity; at some point you will just know that all you need to do to go to alpha is to will it so. This is what I do—I just will it to be. You can buy instruments that signal you when you reach alpha and theta, but I don't recommend them for two reasons. First, they are expensive, and second, the instructions in the next several paragraphs place you always in control and independent of any gadget. My thrust is to enable you to be totally self-sufficient and independent.

When you become as skilled at self-hypnosis as I've described, program yourself so that you will be able to go to theta whenever you enter your room and then count down from ten to one as you visualize the numbers.

After you have done the ten to one countdown in your room, attempt to retrieve some specific information or make a specific contact. You should have planned the specific project in advance (make it a rather simple project to begin with). If you succeed, you have reached theta. If not, continue programming and trying daily until you ultimately succeed— and you will succeed if you do not give up. Sometimes, you will not get your answer immediately, but if you did reach theta, you will receive it within seventy-two hours.

Once, I needed to consult with higher intelligence for some direction in a personal matter. Nothing happened, and I knew I was in theta. The next day while driving my car I was suddenly visited with the intelligence I had sought. The key words are: Patience, Perseverance, and Practice.

Literally, the world is at your command if you want to develop your skills high enough to make it happen. Go as far as you wish. It is your choice.

SUMMARY

You have examined a great many hypnosis routines—long ones and short ones. You have read case histories and the routines used. You have read examples of improvising and modifying routines and sequences, and probably have the idea of modifying and improvising pretty well clear in your mind.

Following are some important points I want you to keep in mind.

The hypnosis routines in this book are ones I use. They are good and they work, but there are hundreds of others that work just as well. Each hypnotist develops his or her own routines and sequences.

Use the routines in this book to help you get started and master your skills, but do not feel locked into them. Feel free to alter, change, or eliminate as you see fit, in light of your own increasing knowledge and experience.

Improvising is limited only by your imagination—use self-hypnosis to expand your own imagination.

Use visualization to achieve results. In chapter 10 I had the little girl with the earache create a third eye and look at her ear from the inside. Then she lit up her ear like an electric light in a cave. Often the more unusual or bizarre your visualization techniques, the more effective the results. Do not restrict yourself by conventional thinking. Unfetter your mind.

The one important caution: Always use positive, constructive statements in your routines and suggestions. Always say what you want, and not what you don't want. For example, if you are helping a woman overcome her fear of water by having her visualize herself swimming. You might say,

"Now visualize yourself wading out into the water. It is warm and relaxing. It is a beautiful day and you are happy. You lean forward in the water and gently stroke your way across the pool. It is a good feeling. You are a good swimmer....."

Do not say,

"You won't drown because you are a good swimmer."

Or,

"Don't be afraid, the water isn't deep."

Use of the words *drown* and *afraid* automatically condition the subject to expect the worst, and you will reinforce the fear rather than get rid of it. So think your words through very carefully before using them. Another key word to avoid is can't.

Whenever I program for something, I always conclude with: *And with harm to no one.* I recommend that you do the same. You don't want to achieve something that could cause harm to others or to yourself.

You now posses knowledge of what is perhaps the most valuable self-enrichment tool in the world today. There is only one thing remaining to do:

Close your eyes, take a deep breath, and....

GET OUT OF YOUR WAY

Unlocking the Power of Your Mind to Get What You Want

Layton Park

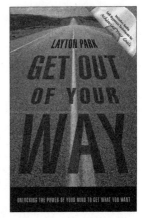

Beliefs, dreams, fears, goals—they all begin in the mind. Hypnosis offers a way to tap into the subconscious mind to produce amazing life changes.

From professional sports to the business world, hypnosis has helped millions achieve their desires. In Get Out of Your Way, Layton Park explains how and why hypnosis works, and shares "universal laws of mind" for transforming our belief system to allow our dreams to come true. Readers will learn how to clarify goals, construct effective affirmations, and engage these affirmations for positive life-changing results. Also featured are compelling case histories—true stories from the author—demonstrating the success of self-hypnosis.

Included with the book is an audio CD of easy-to-follow self-hypnosis techniques that can be used for accomplishing career goals, losing weight, quitting smoking, resolving phobias, and fulfilling a wide variety of personal ambitions.

0-7387-1052-0, 240 pp., 6 x 9, softcover   **$21.95**

PRACTICAL GUIDE TO CREATIVE VISUALIZATION

Manifest Your Desires

Denning & Phillips

All things you will ever want must have their start in your mind. The average person uses very little of the full creative power that is his or hers, potentially. It's like the power locked in the atom—it's all there, but you have to learn to release it and apply it constructively.

Some people apply this innate power without actually knowing what they are doing, and achieve great success and happiness; most people, however, use this same power, again unknowingly, incorrectly, and experience bad luck, failure, or at best an unfulfilled life.

This book changes that. Through an easy series of step-by-step, progressive exercises, your mind is applied to bring desire into realization! Wealth, power, success, happiness, even psychic powers...even what we call magickal power and spiritual attainment...all can be yours. You can easily develop this completely natural power, and correctly apply it, for your immediate and practical benefit. Illustrated with unique, "puts-you-into-the-picture" visualization aids.

0–87542–183–0, 294 pp., 5 ¼ x 8, illus.   **$10.95**

SELF HYPNOSIS FOR A BETTER LIFE

William W. Hewitt

The sound of your own voice is an incredibly powerful tool for speaking to and reprogramming your subconscious. Now, for the first time, you can select your own self-hypnosis script and record it yourself. *Self-Hypnosis for a Better Life* gives the exact wording for 23 unique situations that can be successfully handled with self-hypnosis. Each script is complete in itself and only takes 30 minutes to record. You simply read the script aloud into a tape recorder, then replay the finished tape back to yourself and reap the rewards of self-hypnosis!

Whether you want to eradicate negativity from your life, attract a special romantic partner, solve a problem, be more successful at work, or simply relax, you will find a number of tapes to suit your needs. Become your own hypnotherapist as you design your own self-improvement program, and you can make anything happen.

1-56718-358-1, 5 ³⁄₁₆ x 8   **$11.95**

256 pp., illus., softcover

PSYCHIC DEVELOPMENT FOR BEGINNERS

An Easy Guide to Releasing and Developing Your Psychic Abilities

William W. Hewitt

Psychic Development for Beginners provides detailed instruction on developing your sixth sense, or psychic ability. Improve your sense of worth, your sense of responsibility and therefore your ability to make a difference in the world. Innovative exercises like "The Skyscraper" allow beginning students of psychic development to quickly realize personal and material gain through their own natural talent.

Benefits range from the practical to spiritual. Find a parking space anywhere, handle a difficult salesperson, choose a compatible partner, and even access different time periods! Practice psychic healing on pets or humans—and be pleasantly surprised by your results. Use psychic commands to prevent dozing while driving. Preview out-of-body travel, cosmic consciousness, and other alternative realities. Instruction in *Psychic Development for Beginners* is supported by personal anecdotes, 44 psychic development exercises, and 28 related psychic case studies to help students gain a comprehensive understanding of the psychic realm.

1-56718-360-3, 5 ¼ x 8, 216 pp., softcover $11.95

WRITE YOUR OWN MAGIC

Richard Webster

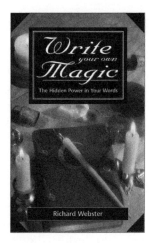

Write your innermost dreams and watch them come true! This book will show you how to use the incredible power of words to create the life that you have always dreamed about. We all have desires, hopes and wishes. Sadly, many people think theirs are unrealistic or unattainable. Write Your Own Magic shows you how to harness these thoughts by putting them to paper.

Once a dream is captured in writing it becomes a goal, and your subconscious mind will find ways to make it happen. From getting a date for Saturday night to discovering your purpose in life, you can achieve your goals, both small and large. You will also learn how to speed up the entire process by making a ceremony out of telling the universe what it is you want. With the simple instructions in this book, you can send your energies out into the world and magnetize all that is happiness, success, and fulfillment to you.

- Send your energies out into the universe with rituals, ceremonies, and spells
- Magnetize yourself so that your desires are attracted to you, while the things you do not want are repelled
- Create suitable spells for different purposes
- Produce quick money, attract a lover, harness the powers of protection, win that job promotion

0-7387-0001-0
5 ³⁄₁₆ x 8, 312 pp.   **$12.95**

NEW AGE HYPNOSIS

Dr. Bruce Goldberg

"This is simply the most easy-to-use and complete system of self-hypnosis available without a prescription."
—Dr. Bruce Goldberg

NEW AGE
HYPNOSIS

DR. BRUCE GOLDBERG

We spend seven hours of every 24-hour day in natural hypnosis. This affords us a tremendous opportunity to grow spiritually, if only we could learn to maximize this state.

Now you can, with the most comprehensive self-hypnosis program available. Under the guidance of a trained and experienced hypnotherapist, you will learn how to place yourself into a hypnotic trance and experience various metaphysical approaches from past life regression to superconscious mind taps, out-of-body experiences, and soul plane ascension techniques. You can also learn how to become a New Age hypnotherapist, if you so desire.

Upon completion of this book, you will understand hypnosis, its characteristics and stages. You will be able to induce a hypnotic trance, deepen it, maximize a clinically beneficial state, and return to the normal waking state a more spiritually evolved soul.

1–56718–320–4, 240 pp., 6 x 9   **$14.95**

JOURNEY OF SOULS
Case Studies of Life Between Lives

Michael Newton, Ph.D.

This remarkable book uncovers—for the first time—the mystery of life in the spirit world after death on earth. Dr. Michael Newton, a hypnotherapist in private practice, has developed his own hypnosis technique to reach his subjects' hidden memories of the hereafter. The narrative is woven as a progressive travel log around the accounts of twenty-nine people who were placed in a state of super-consciousness. While in deep hypnosis, these subjects describe what has happened to them between their former reincarnations on earth. They reveal graphic details about how it feels to die, who meets us right after death, what the spirit world is really like, where we go and what we do as souls, and why we choose to come back in certain bodies.

After reading *Journey of Souls,* you will acquire a better understanding of the immortality of the human soul. Plus, you will meet day-to-day personal challenges with a greater sense of purpose as you begin to understand the reasons behind events in your own life.

1-56718-485-5, 288 pp., 6 x 9, illus.   **$14.95**